Memoirs & Miracles

Janet. I. Edwards

Memoirs & Miracles

Janet I. Edwards

Edwards Publications
2010

Edwards Publications.
61 Chaigley Road, Longridge, Preston PR3 3TQ.

Photograph on title page by Val Hatton

Preparatory copy-editing and typesetting
By Sharon Beck

British Library Cataloguing in Publication Data.
A record of this book is available from the British Library.

ISBN: 978-0-9563671-0-5

Typeset by RefineCatch Ltd, Bungay, Suffolk

Printed in Great Britain by:
Cambrian Printers, Aberystwyth

Contents

List of Photographs

Preface

Having experienced so many miracles in my own life as well as witnessing miracles of transformation in other lives, these have often been a topic of conversation. But one day, almost nine years ago, I felt the strongest prompting to share these miracles more widely. I believed that prompting was of God and wondered if it meant that I should write a book; so I began. Although other things soon encroached on the time set aside, the conviction has never left me. So, more recently, I returned to the task and here is the result.

My hope and prayer is that it will be a blessing and a source of encouragement to all who read it.

Janet I. Edwards.

One

Early Years

Nestling in the heart of the South Derbyshire countryside lies the village of Coton-in-the-Elms. It was here, on 6th February 1934, that I was born, the first child of Nance and Frank and the first grandchild of Nellie and Harold Coates, who lived next door, my maternal grandparents and the only grandparents I ever knew. They were to have a formative influence on my life.

My early days were carefree, even idyllic. Growing up amongst green fields and towering elm trees, being free to roam the countryside with no fear of being molested, enjoying simple pastimes such as whip and top, skipping, bat and ball, hop-scotch, tag, climbing trees, cricket, football and the like, were blessings taken for granted.

The seasons brought their own particular pleasures. Through spring into summer wild flowers grew in profusion. In the meadows we found speedwell, buttercups, daisies, ladysmocks, cow-slips, harebells and clover, to name but a few. From the boggy areas huge, yellow kingcups smiled up at us and in the banks along the hedgerows the shy violet drooped its head. The hedges themselves were alive as the birds built their nests and reared their fledglings. What a delight actually to see the clutch of turquoise speckled eggs in the blackbird's nest or the speckled greyish-white eggs in the robin's nest and later to see the young emerge! The young lambs frolicked in the fields; new life was everywhere. The scent of new-mown hay added to the breath of heady Spring and in this, too, we played our part. The farmers were glad of all the help they could muster for these were the days of sweat and toil. Those of us who were a little older than our younger siblings were trusted to wield a pitch-fork and toss the stooks of hay on to the waiting trailer. We had our reward as we rode home on top of the load. And always a welcome sight was the return of the swallows. The mellow notes of the blackbird's song, the repetitive but melodious tunes of the thrush, the trill of the rising skylark, the call of the cuckoo, blending with so many more were the welcome symphony of Summer.

From the streams we would pick fresh watercress and as autumn approached we delighted in finding the first mushrooms in the fields. The hedgerows yielded their harvest of beech-nuts, hazelnuts and blackberries and, with hands scratched and stained, we carried them into the kitchen.

The days seemed shorter, the nights longer, but we settled into the evening around a cosy, coal fire, with our jig-saw puzzles and cross-words, or perhaps relaxed with our favourite radio programme, "Dick Barton, Special Agent". On occasions we gathered around the harmonium to sing a few hymns and songs. Soon winter was upon us – and we had some real winters! I well remember the one of 1947 when we were walking on hard-packed snow over the tops of the hedges. When the ponds froze over quite hard the sliding and skating began and we fell over each other with great delight in spite of the pain. Yes, I shall always be glad of my country childhood.

We lived next door to my grandparents. Grandad was a cripple due to an injury sustained in the coal-mine and in those days there was no compensation. He was, even so, very active. He could move around a little with the help of two walking sticks, had a wheel-chair and also a motorised chair. He was the village bandmaster and the Coton Silver Prize band had competed very ably at national level.

When I was nine years old he asked me if I would like to play the cornet. I was thrilled and began to learn under his expert tuition. I seem to remember one of my first pieces being "Rule Britannia" so I must have been doing very well! Soon I was playing third cornet in the brass band. But this was not all. Grandad was an exceptional musician, being proficient on organ and piano as well as able to play and teach the whole range of brass band instruments, but he also played the tenor saxophone and with this he led a dance band, named "The Harmonic Four". It was not long before I was part of this, too, and most Saturday evenings saw us at some local village dance-hall. I think I was fairly well-paid too as I received ten shillings each time! Converted to fifty pence that doesn't sound a big deal but in those days it went a long way. Not only so, but I received much praise, especially from the American soldiers, for this was the time of the second world war and their shouts of "Swell!" and gifts of chewing gum were very acceptable.

I don't know that grandad had received any formal musical training, yet he wrote and arranged music and passed his skills on to others. I still have a copy of a song he wrote about the Home Guard; at least he wrote the music and a friend of his wrote the words and it was duly published. Soon I began piano lessons and it seemed that music was to play a big part in my life.

Gran was a wonderful person, practical, down to earth and no nonsense but a deeply caring, self-effacing person who lived for others. She had had to face hard times, especially with grandad's incapacity, but between them they were great achievers. At one time they had a fish and chip business, at another they made and sold ice-cream and in my childhood they kept the village post office and grocery store. I usually had a few sweets in my pocket, even during the war years and I always seemed to have plenty of friends! Grandad managed the post office for as long as he could and I'm sure he brightened people's lives with his sense of fun. Gran managed the shop and listened to people's problems! Grandad also had a workshop and a wood-turning lathe and was very skilled in producing candlesticks, cake-stands and the like. He made a desk for me, which I still have, and a crane for my brother. The lathe was a treadle lathe and I spent many happy hours treadling the lathe while grandad worked with his chisels and gouges. In fact I think I spent more time at gran and grandad's than I did at home. Mum was often there, too, giving a helping hand

Life wasn't easy for mum. Dad's fondness for alcohol, which I think was, in part, a reaction against a strict Methodist background, caused us no little heartache especially as he could become violent. This was mainly at weekends, after Friday payday! But I suspect it caused financial problems too. Yet by nature he was warm and loving. I remember him coming to mum with a box of chocolates the morning after the night before, perhaps hoping to smooth troubled waters. Mum, however, was a strong character and not one to be walked over so there were tensions. But gran was a tower of strength and I suspect did more for us than I shall ever know.

My brother, Graham, was five years younger than me and as his big sister and somewhat of a tom-boy I was his chief protector. If he was bullied then I was on the war-path! It was not that he couldn't stand up for himself but he was not quite the fighter that his big sister was. In the kitchen, built into one corner, was the copper, underneath which a fire was made each washday to boil the clothes. I would often lift Graham up on to the top of this, not, I hasten to add, when the fire was kindled, so that I could comb and style, as I thought, his hair. He had a natural wave in the front which I wanted to train. Even then, I think, I had aspirations to become a hairdresser, but that was not to be.

When I was ten years old I had to face my first bereavement. Granddad died after quite a lengthy illness, which I think was the result of his earlier accident, at the age of 49 years. It was a great blow to the whole family, especially to my mother and gran. I was very close to him and I so wanted to attend the funeral, but it was in February and in the depths of a white winter, and it was thought best that I should not go. What a great sorrow that was to me.

Music had been such a big part of grandad's life that mum and gran could not bear to hear music in the house. This meant the end of my piano lessons and my cornet fastened in its case. It was like being in a black prison. I can't remember how long it was before I began again to tinkle on the piano and dared to blow my cornet. I know the vicar asked one day if I could help out on the church organ; he was musical and said he would help me but I think he must have been pretty desperate! Although we belonged to the Methodist chapel and I was a regular attender at the Sunday School in the days when we stayed in our own camps, I did give some help and benefited from the experience. So music was again seen to be part of my life but, sadly, no regular piano or cornet lessons in these vital years.

I think I was taken to the Methodist Sunday School before I attended day-school. Faith and Fred, a married couple, and Faith's sister, Jennie, were the teachers in what was then a thriving Sunday-School. The highlights were, I suppose, the prize-giving, the Sunday School anniversary and the annual outing, often to the sea-side and usually to Skegness, Mablethorpe or Cleethorpes which were the nearest. The Sunday-School anniversary was a village event; most families had children or grand-children in the Sunday-School and all would be wearing their new outfits. Faith was the organist and trained the children for the Anniversary and I must say they did her proud. Parts had been learned, songs well-rehearsed, and recitations committed to memory – mostly! But the week by week faithful teaching of Bible stories and spiritual values and the times of prayer and worship brought a real sense of the presence of God because those who taught us knew His presence in their own lives. Imbibing this atmosphere was to influence some of us greatly and me in particular. I know that our Sunday School teachers prayed for us that we would discover for ourselves the presence of God and commit our lives to His service. One Sunday afternoon their prayers for me were answered. Our two o' clock service was conducted by two full-time workers from the inter-denominational Derbyshire Village Mission, two ladies who preached about God's love for us all, demonstrated in the life, death and resurrection of Jesus Christ and the need for us to respond to that love and accept the free gift of forgiveness and eternal life. That day, September 21st 1947 was a turning point in my life as I stayed behind after the service and accepted Jesus Christ as my own Saviour and Lord. That, I believe, is the greatest miracle God has worked in my life, though many more were to follow. Even then there were many other influences that could have turned my life in quite different directions and I was certainly conscious of my need of forgiveness and strength to live as I was meant to.

Two

Called to Serve

I was glad of the counsel of those who led me to faith in Christ. "Remember," they said, after I had committed my life to Him, "if you are tempted to doubt that anything real happened, count on the promise of Jesus in Revelation 3 verse 20, 'I stand at the door and knock. If any man hear my voice and open the door, I will come in.'" I did count on that and began to live by faith rather than depending on feelings to indicate the presence and activity of God. I also took on board the advice that to grow as a Christian I needed to develop my own devotional life of prayer and Bible-reading as well as to have fellowship with other Christians. As a young Christian I was in the minority in our village chapel but I have to say that the fellowship there enriched me greatly and some of those older Christians were a great help to me.

So I grew as a Christian. I had battles to fight and temptations to face and sometimes I didn't do too well in these, but I learned to trust in the power of Jesus and so win through. I remember being challenged as I read in my Bible about our bodies being temples of the Holy Spirit. I was hooked on cigarettes in my early teens and although there was then no firm evidence of the effects of smoking on health I was unhappy about the habit. One day as I stood in the kitchen I suddenly found myself saying, “I can’t deal with this, Lord, but I believe You can” and I claimed His power in this temptation. In view of what happened later in my life, I’m glad I did.

More and more I wanted my life to count for something, to be used to bring glory to God and I began to ask Him what He wanted me to do and to direct me in His way. I believe God has a plan for each life and I wanted His plan for mine to be worked through.

I enjoyed school and in the village elementary school did very well in most things. At secondary school maths seemed a little harder but French I took to as a duck to water. Later there were choices to be made. The idea of becoming a teacher had great appeal and when I finally made applications to colleges I had to decide what should be my main subject. The French teacher was convinced it should be French and the music master adamant that I should major in music. I loved both, though my choice would have been music had I not missed out in my earlier years when piano and brass tuition ceased. So, armed with my French books I went to college, but somehow, after a few lectures, didn’t have quite the same enthusiasm as I had had in school. Then I found myself in conversation with the music lecturer who seemed to know it was one of the loves of my life. “Come with me,” she said and took me to the piano where she proceeded to give me numerous ear tests. “I’ll take you,” she said, and so I switched to music with some hard work ahead on trumpet and keyboard. But it was all in the plan, though I didn't know then how God intended to use these musical skills later on.

After college I taught in Primary School for three years and enjoyed it immensely though I sensed God's purposes unfolding still and felt He was leading – I was not quite sure where. I was, however, very sure that He was calling me to preach and so, after further study, I became a Methodist local preacher. Paul's words to Timothy, "Do the work of an evangelist" seemed to be God's words to me. But in what context? In personal witness and conversation, of course, as it should be for every Christian, for we are meant to share our faith. But I wanted to give my whole life in this way.

I had spoken about this to a missionary whose advice was that I should get some experience in the workaday world and God would make His way plain. I then spoke to our own minister. Of course, the ministry then was a male domain but he asked if I had not thought about the Wesley Deaconess Order. I had never even heard of it! When he eventually gave me some information about it and I read about deaconess work in big city missions, though there were many other areas of work, I was not too thrilled. When I read that deaconesses wore a uniform with stiff collar and cuffs and a hat, to boot, I really thought that was not me and put the information leaflets in the side-board drawer to gather dust. But God doesn't give up on us or let our prejudices stand in the way if we really want to know His will.

Later, we were to have a mission in our village, centred on the chapel. We learned it was to be led by two Methodist deaconesses whose home and base would be a Home Missions caravan, though the meetings would be held in the chapel. And we prayed that God would use them in our village, that people would be converted and added to our fellowship. Yes, we really prayed and we knew the people in whose lives we would like to see God at work!

Then the day came when the deaconesses were due to arrive and hold the opening meeting. I'm not quite sure what my expectations were, but I think I had a mental picture of two rather staid, elderly ladies. Imagine my surprise at the revelation of two young women full of the joy of serving Jesus. This was my first meeting with Sister Kitty Foster and Sister Margaret Birch. I was to discover how normal and approachable they were and eventually to count them as my friends.

Yes, we had a good mission and as they moved on to other churches in the district I was invited to join them and take part in some of their meetings. And guess who God was speaking to – yes, He was speaking to me – "This is the way; walk in it." And if I needed extra confirmation that this was the way it had been given during the mission in our church when mum had surrendered her life to Christ. I knew she hadn't wanted me to leave home again but now I knew that she was prepared for me to go with her blessing. So I offered for the Wesley Deaconess Order.

Perhaps here I should give some information about the Order and what was involved in belonging to it. Deaconesses, of course, go much further back than Methodism. We understand from the New Testament that there were those who ministered as deaconesses in the early Church; the two words, 'minister' and 'deaconess', in fact, actually sprang from the same root, a word which means 'servant'.

In the eighteen hundreds an Order of deaconesses was brought into being by Pastor Theodor Fliedner at Kaiserswerth on the Rhine and this spread widely on the Continent. During a visit to Germany, Dr. T. B. Stephenson observed their work and was so impressed that in 1890 he founded the Wesley Deaconess Order in the Wesleyan Church. Soon a similar Order was founded by Rev. T. J. Cope in the United Methodist Free Church, and soon afterwards there were deaconesses also in the Primitive Methodist Church. Training was initially for one year, after which deaconesses were appointed by the Warden. In the early 1900s they received an allowance of £25 per year in addition to board and lodging. With the Methodist Union of 1932 the Orders became one, the Wesley Deaconess Order of the Methodist Church.

From the beginning the Sisters were involved in pastoral, teaching and evangelistic work and the scope of the work grew. Some were appointed to full-time youth work, some to Social and Moral Welfare Work, some to Industrial chaplaincies, some to overseas missionary work, and the scope of the work continued to grow as, indeed, it does now.

When Dr. Stephenson founded the Order he laid down certain principles as follows:

1. There must be vocation, but no vow.
2. There must be discipline without servility.

3. There must be association not excluding freedom.

Furthermore, it was to be a celibate Order.

Over the years Conference passed various resolutions to extend the scope and work of deaconesses and in 1936 a service for the Ordination of Deaconesses was officially accepted.

When I offered for the Order in 1957 all deaconesses were trained at Ilkley in Yorkshire for a period of two years, after which there followed two years of probation, prior to Ordination.

It was to Ilkley I went for an interview. Not only did we face a full committee of thirty plus ministers and deaconesses, all in dark suits or navy uniforms, but also had a one to one conversation with a senior deaconess. She made clear the demands of the work as well as its privileges, in particular stressing the issue of celibacy.

A few days later we would receive a letter indicating the decision of the Committee. I was so thrilled that in my case the decision was in the affirmative. All deaconesses were expected to intend life service and if life service was to be life service, then in those days marriage was out of the question.

Prior to my offer I had already ended a courtship of one year. I was very sure of where God's call lay. Yet I had no financial backing and my parents were certainly not well off. My minister's advice had been that I should wait a few years and save towards my training but my certainty of God's call urged me forward. I well remember the day, some months later, when the Warden of the Order called me into his office and presented me with a package containing an anonymous gift of money. God is no man's debtor and has His own wonderful ways of supplying our need.

College was good for me. We were a mixed bunch of student deaconesses: some of us were extrovert, others reserved, and I think that we all had different perspectives on things like worship, theology and even the Scriptures. It was quite a steep learning curve to accept and appreciate those who were very different from me and it was quite a challenge and privilege to share with these same people a common love for Jesus and a common life in the Spirit. Lectures in Old and New Testament, theology, church history, evangelism and pastoral work as well as practical work each week in surrounding areas and churches were all part of our training. We did our share of housework, too, deemed to be a very necessary discipline and preparation for the future. But there were also times of fun and celebration and we were all very much enriched by our times of shared prayer and worship.

Of course, we made our own particular friends. Helen came to college as I began my second year and her home was in Scotland. It would have been rather a long way for her to travel for a half-term break so she came home with me to south Derbyshire. Dad always had a soft spot for attractive ladies and really took to Helen. He still had his drink problem, though we saw no evidence of that during half-term.

However, I felt I should have asked how things were and returned to college feeling I had failed in my witness. Imagine my surprise when, a few days later, a letter arrived – from dad! This was a first as mum usually wrote the letters. He wrote to say that he had been greatly challenged while we were home for half-term to see how happy we were in our obedience to God's call. That night he had spent three and a half hours on his knees, battling with God and finally had committed his life to Christ.

When he came from work the next day and told mum, "I've finished with drink," her reply, not surprisingly, was, "Oh yes, I've heard that before". But God had worked a miracle and my prayers of ten years had been wonderfully answered. As I walked around college that day it was like walking on air. I must admit that when Helen eventually went to work in the Gambia I felt pretty low but God always provides for each step of the journey.

After two years in training I was to go into my first appointment – please, not city missions, Lord! Well, it could have been in a country circuit working with ministers or in the forces in chaplaincy work or in a number of other areas, but I was still sure that God had called me to be an evangelist. Indeed, this was confirmed yet again as I was told that I was to go on Caravan Mission work. And so I was sent to Lancashire and worked with another deaconess for the whole of that year in the North Lancs District. I had a number of years on Caravan Mission work and what wonderful years they were.

1. Janet on tricycle

2. Coton-in-the-Elms Methodist Church – Janet's spiritual home

Three

Caravan Missions

At that time there were six caravans supported by the Methodist Home Missions department with names like “Enterprise”, “Joy” and “Liberator”, each staffed by two deaconesses. The general pattern was that a caravan was sent to a district for a year and moved to different circuits throughout the district for short-term missions. Many of these circuits were country circuits and I was thrilled to be working in the villages.

The mornings were spent in preparation for meetings and in various chores, followed by a prayer fellowship at twenty to ten when local folk came and shared. I suppose it had always been at that time on all the caravans and very often the prayer fellowship continued in the village after the caravan had moved on, so twenty to ten became a very special time. The afternoons were for visiting and every effort was made to visit every house as well as to find convenient times to visit pubs, workplaces, schools or any other venue where we could meet people. Evenings saw us meeting with the children at about 6.00 p.m. and running an adult meeting at about 7.30 p.m. In the early days I had a piano accordion that came into its own for children's meetings and open-air work. Later, when guitars became popular I made it my business to learn and use that too. The teenagers were not forgotten; the youth squash, usually on Friday evenings, saw a crowd of young people meeting in the caravan, often with many questions wide and deep!

Some people wondered why we had left behind a secure and comparatively well-paid job like teaching for one where we received an allowance rather than a salary, just about enough to make ends meet. But obeying God's call brings its own rewards. Our needs were met in many wonderful ways and the thrill of serving Him in missions was far more wonderful than working to amass a fortune. Indeed, these years were good for us. We had no home to furnish, no furniture to carry around, no removal costs to worry about and the caravan was moved from place to place for us. We were able to travel light and give ourselves to the work of the Kingdom.

During my three years' teaching my mode of transport had been a motor-cycle. My first was a B.S.A. Bantam Major 150 cc. soon to be followed by a B.S.A. 250 cc. I took great delight in pulling into a petrol station where, usually, in those days, you were served by an assistant, and hearing him say, "Yes sir?" Well, how was he to know that inside the leather jacket and other gear was a lady! I enjoyed my motor-cycling days immensely. My B.S.A. 250 cc went with me to deaconess college and into the work.

I began that first year of caravan mission in Lancashire in the Clitheroe circuit. The caravan was to be sited in the village of West Bradford and we were to mission there as well as in the villages of Grindleton and Waddington. I rode into West Bradford and stopped at the Post Office. "Could you tell me please where the Methodist Chapel is and if there is a caravan parked there?" I asked the lady behind the counter. "Yes," she replied, "and we're part of your flock." The words were music to my ears. We were to get to know Mrs. Rushton and her two unmarried daughters, Lizzie and Mary, very well over the coming weeks and months. Mary soon became my favourite cook and Lizzie shared her love of the Ribble Valley, especially through the many photographs she had taken. Indeed, she presented me with an album before I left which I still have. The photographs were black and white, of course, but beautifully clear. The large, walnut piano that stood in their living room was my delight. No-one in the family played it but they were always glad when I did. Mrs. Rushton outlived her two daughters and on her death the piano was willed to me. I was so thrilled. It has travelled with me to many places where I have lived and ministered and is one of my greatest treasures.

Living now in the Ribble Valley it has been good to renew contact with people I met some forty-five years ago during caravan missions. Those missions were fruitful, often bringing new life to individuals and congregations. Sometimes there were visible results as people heard the good news and made their own personal response of faith. There were those for whom it was an initial response to Jesus Christ and a definite commitment to His service. This happened for young and old alike. For some it was during one of the mission meetings, for others it was a more private affair, perhaps after discussion and prayer and much consideration. It was both thrilling and humbling to witness such experiences or be told about them. Perhaps we didn't know the half of what God was doing in people's lives.

One of the great joys over the years has been to witness the growth and development of faith in the lives of those who were influenced by those caravan missions. There will always be those who express doubt about the value of such missions and about commitment made during such missions. "Will the commitment last?" "Is the change real?" "Is it not merely an emotional experience?" Perhaps we have all met those who question so. For some who come to faith emotion also plays its part as it does in many other areas of life. But a considered response, a real acceptance of God's offer of salvation, a putting down roots in personal prayer and meditation as well as in fellowship with other Christians are always encouraged and where these things are practised there is the development of a strong faith and a real experience of God. We sing with Charles Wesley, "My Jesus to know and feel His blood flow, 'tis life everlasting, 'tis heaven below".

Our first meeting of the mission was usually one in which we were welcomed by the minister and people of the churches whom we would be serving. I well remember one such meeting at Mereside in the Blackpool South circuit, during that year in North Lancashire. Rev. Clifford Laidlow was the superintendent minister and led the meeting. He seemed to me a man of deep spirituality and had visited the estate prior to our arrival. It was his birthday and he told us that he had two birthdays, the day when he was born into this world and the day when he began life afresh with Jesus. That theme ran through the meeting that concluded with a time of open prayer. One lady, Mrs. Lee, whose prayer I remember so vividly, had been visited by Clifford Laidlow and had come to church at his invitation. This was her first appearance in church since childhood. In a broad Lancashire accent she prayed, “Thank you, Lord, for my second birthday today: that’s all I can say, Amen.” I don’t think I’ve heard a more moving prayer than that since. That night was a wonderful turning point in her life. She came to the meetings, took part in the morning prayer fellowship in the caravan and grew in her new-found faith. I remember her saying, “I’m sixty-eight but I feel life’s just beginning!” Some years later I returned to Mereside to see if Mrs. Lee were still there. I was told by the church steward, “No, she died of cancer a short time ago but she had a radiant faith right up to the end.” That was enough for me to know.

The following year brought a change of colleague. I was to continue on caravan mission work, but this time with Olive and in an area new to me, South Devon in the Plymouth and Exeter district. By this time I had exchanged my motorcyle for a car, but only to appease my parents. My own thoughts had been on exchanging the 250 cc B.S.A. for a 350 cc Triumph Twin, but my mother pleaded with me, “Please let us help you get a little car.” So they did. It was a Standard 8 with a fairly high mileage and had been a firm's car. The difference between driving a car and a motorcycle was unbelievable. I felt as though I was crawling round the bends in the road. However, I tested it to its limits and tried to push it further! I think Olive's heart often missed a few beats as she rode beside me.

So we arrived in the Kingsbridge circuit, new territory to us both and missioned in the villages of Modbury and Aveton Gifford. There again it was our joy to see people responding to the Gospel. Ann made her personal commitment to Jesus during that year and we were to get to know Ann and her husband, Norman, who was already a Christian, and count them as our friends. We spent some happy hours on their farm and often enjoyed a crab supper which was quite a ritual every Saturday night for Norman.

Mrs. Ellis lived in Aveton Gifford and I think I remember rightly that she was in her seventies when she made her commitment to Jesus. It can happen at any stage of life and is always wonderful to witness but I am always so glad that I was led to take this step when I was just in my teens. Now I am able to look back on a life of Christian growth and service, able to recall so much Scripture through which God has guided and strengthened me and able to see the unfolding of God's plan for my life. There is absolutely nothing more worthwhile than living for Jesus. And, of course, there is always more to look forward to, ultimately, of course, heaven itself.

I'm not quite sure how we got into the Bampton circuit in Somerset during this year or where, exactly, this mission slotted into our itinerary, but I well remember missioning in Petton and Clayhanger. The caravan was sited in the Venner's farmyard. This delightful couple had a number of grown up sons who worked hard on the farm. When they came in for breakfast each morning we were invited to join them. What a spread! Mrs. Venner had made fresh cream and the table was spread fit for a king. Porridge, cereal, eggs, bacon, liver, kidneys, heart, toast, butter and more were all available each morning. I wonder we were able to do any work for the rest of the day or to eat another meal, but I guess we did; we were much younger then.

Doris was a member at Clayhanger and a Sunday School teacher there. I remember her making a personal commitment to Jesus. "Now" she said, "I shall know the one I'm talking to the children about." These commitments were so real. I had the joy of meeting Doris and some of the other members at Petton Chapel years later. We had all grown older and had faced some of life's trials, but had known God's grace and strength.

In the Totnes area we missioned in the villages of Harberton and Harbertonford. We had some great fellowship in the whole area with a number of Brethren believers and really appreciated their support. One young man in particular we were to get to know very well. George visited the caravan and came to a number of meetings. He had a lovely tenor voice and it was a joy to sing with him. He played the organ at the Methodist Chapel and was one of the leaders in the Brethren Fellowship. So he was very committed to the Lord's service. We were in many ways very alike and a bond grew between us. It was not long before George was showing me some of the beauty spots of the area; the Old Clapper Bridge on Dartmoor, particularly beautiful in the moonlight, Start Point and Prawle Point, Slapton Sands and many other lovely places. I visited his home and he visited mine. We wondered if God had a plan for us to be together and, of course, we made it a matter of prayer.

The missions continued throughout the year. We moved on to a housing estate in the Plymouth area where the going was tough for the people at the chapel and, indeed, it was on the cards that it might close. However, God used that mission to light and rekindle faith in people's hearts and there was a new spirit abroad. The chapel did not close and when the caravan moved on the prayer meeting continued. We went also over the border into Cornwall into the lovely Tamar valley where we missioned in St. Anne's Chapel and Albaston. Some of these Cornish chapels were huge and very difficult for the people to maintain. But, again, God moved amongst us and people were blessed and encouraged. It was the responsibility of the circuit to move the caravan on to its next place of mission, so after we had carefully packed everything away we had a welcome three day break. On one of these I suggested to Olive that we drive up to my home in Derbyshire. She really thought I couldn't be serious. There was no motorway then and the drive up the old Fosseway took about eight hours. But indeed I was serious. I was a home-bird and I am one still. Olive's home was in Leeds so that really was out of the question for a three-day break. Well, it was as good as I anticipated it would be and I think Olive enjoyed it too.

That was a good year and one, for me, of God's confirmation of my call to the Deaconess Order. George felt constrained to stay in Devon and give himself to the work there and I knew God was leading me on in the service of the Methodist Church and the work of evangelism. That year, 1962, should have been my Ordination year but this had been deferred until the way seemed clear. All deaconesses had two years' training followed by two years on probation. If, at the end of this period, the Order and the deaconess felt it right, Ordination followed. Some of us took a little longer! Now I could look forward to Ordination in 1963.

Olive and I had a further year together on the caravan but this time the pattern of working was quite different. Whilst deaconesses on other caravans continued to do short term missions, we had what I think was an experimental year. Instead of spending the whole year in one District we were sent to various parts of the country and often for longer periods. There was a mission in Derbyshire, another in the lovely little village of Wilton in Somerset and a period in the Bridport circuit focussing on the chapels in West Bay and Burton Bradstock. In West Bay we saw something that we had never seen before and that, I think, neither of us has seen since. We were told to go down to the beach at a particular time of day and there would be sprats galore lying on the sand. So we did. The beach was silver with sprats that had been chased in by the mackerel, a wonderful sight and, of course, one that illustrated the saying, "set a sprat to catch a mackerel". We filled our buckets and gorged ourselves on sprats, soused and fried. The longest period of this experimental year was a few months on New Parks housing estate in Leicester. The need was for a more concentrated ministry than a short-term mission. We were visited by the local press and able to go into schools and visit around the estate, so people soon knew we were there. It was a time of great encouragement for the church. We became part of the family as we went into the Women's Fellowship, Boy's Brigade, Youth Club and various meetings on the premises as well as preaching on Sundays. Again, lives were touched and people were blessed. But a housing estate is not one of the easiest places in which to serve, and some concentrated, long-term work was needed. And, indeed, this was provided as Olive was sent back the following year to live and work on the estate. So, at the end of two more happy years my first period of ministry on the caravan came to an end. It was a time of fruitful service for which I shall always be thankful.

Four

Circuit Ministry

Part of the discipline of belonging to the Wesley Deaconess Order was to be prepared to go where you were sent. There was not usually any consultation; you were simply directed to your next place and type of service. So, at the end of my two years with Olive, I awaited my marching orders.

Increasingly, with the shortage of ministers, deaconesses were being appointed to circuit work, having pastoral oversight of a number of churches and, in order to fulfil a complete ministry, having a dispensation from Conference to preside at Holy Communion. This was to be my next sphere of service and I was appointed to the Staveley circuit, near Chesterfield. So, September 1962 saw the opening of a new chapter. This was in my native Derbyshire so it was not far from my parents' home in the south of the county. My few goods and chattels were soon installed in the council house which was to be my home.

I had responsibility for four churches: Staveley Zion, New Brimington, Barrow Hill Zion and Barrow Hill Ebenezer, all within just a few miles of each other. There was a good nucleus of committed folk at each church and a good circuit youth fellowship, held after the Sunday evening services in the old Staveley Sunday School. It was encouraging to see up to two hundred young people meeting together. The challenge was to try and remember their names and to help them focus on personal commitment and service. Some, of course, were already committed and enthusiastic. I believe I played my trumpet at the first circuit youth fellowship of the winter in 1962 and the piece was, “It is no secret what God can do.” With youth on my side and music in my blood it wasn’t difficult to get alongside these young people, but I hoped that what would impress and challenge them most would be the difference Jesus made to my life.

Mount Tabor, the New Brimington church, had a good Christian Endeavour and a good nucleus of young people who regularly took part. They also had a lively youth club. So there was plenty to keep me on my toes! Some of these young people were also very active along with the older ones in raising money for the new building fund that was for the provision of a new hall. They asked if they could publish a couple of songs that I had written and sell them for the project. Of course, I was delighted. The first was, “Go on with the Lord” and had just two verses. The second edition also had guitar chords. Apparently it sold very well with repeat orders from as far away as Ireland. The second song was “Not to be lonely but to belong”. These were printed by the young people on an old ink duplicator, but, for all that, were very presentable. Mount Tabor had a lot going for it. Apart from the young people there were some very able and committed members. It was therefore with a tinge of sadness that I lost oversight of the church at the end of the first year, due to circuit realignment. Instead I took Inkersall under my pastoral wing and also moved to live there. There were an increasing number of new houses there and visiting was a priority. I still had the other churches, two at Barrow Hill and one at Staveley. In each place there was a nucleus of faithful, committed people and it was a privilege to share the work with them. At the end of the second year, however, the opportunity came to return to Caravan Missions and, again, bags were packed, farewells said, and it was time to move on.

Something, however, of very special significance had happened in that last year: it was the year of my ordination as a Wesley Deaconess. This had been deferred as I explained in an earlier chapter but now I knew the time was right. Monday, 29th April, 1963, found me, along with five other deaconesses, in Oxford Place Chapel, Leeds, where Rev. Leslie Davison, President of Conference that year, was to conduct our Ordination Service. We were supported by visitors and friends as well as by the rest of the Deaconess Order. This was a very moving and challenging service to which no deaconess came lightly. You will see from the questions asked of each one that there had to be total commitment to God's call. It was an experience I shall never forget and I was deeply moved as we sang the hymn, "Behold the servant of the Lord". The following is the Order of Service for that occasion:

ORDER OF SERVICE

FOR THE ORDINATION OF DEACONESSES

Introductory Worship.

Presentation of the candidates to the President: the names are read out.

The President addresses the candidates and other deaconesses present.

Hymn.

Behold the servant of the Lord.

Then shall the President examine the candidates after the manner following:

Have you duly considered how weighty an undertaking this is, and do you trust that you are inwardly moved by the Holy Ghost to take upon you this office and ministration?

I have so considered and do so trust.

Are you prepared, with a willing mind, to give yourself to this work, and cheerfully and faithfully to perform the service that shall be appointed to you?

I desire so to do, by the help of God.

Will you apply all your diligence to frame and fashion your own life according to the doctrine of Christ; and give yourself to prayer, that you may be made an example to them that believe, in word, in manner of life, in love, in faith, in purity?

I will do so, the Lord being my helper.

The badge of the Order shall then be presented to each candidate. Then, all the candidates kneeling and the people standing, the President, the Warden and a Senior Deaconess, shall lay their hands upon the head of each woman, and the President shall say to each:

Take thou authority to fulfil the office and work of a Deaconess in the Church of God now committed unto thee, in the Name of the Father, and of the Son, and of the Holy Ghost. Amen.

Then shall the President deliver to each candidate a Bible.

Prayer.

More hymns, the President's address and prayers followed. Each of us felt a great sense of the confirmation of our call and a great sense of privilege in being able to serve through the Order. It meant a great deal to see twelve people from my home village, including my parents, in that service and also fifty-two people who had made the journey from Staveley. And I knew that the God who had led me this far would lead me every step of the way.

Five

More Caravan Missions

So my time in the Staveley circuit, brief, but happy, was followed by a return to Caravan Mission work, which thrilled me greatly. Not far away there were two deaconesses conducting Caravan Missions who also knew what their appointments for the following year would be. Edith, who was the senior colleague, was to go to Liverpool for further training in moral and social welfare work. Elizabeth was to remain on the caravan but as yet didn't know who her colleague would be. She knew, however, that I was to go back on the caravan and it occurred to her that we might be sent together. We didn't know each other, though we had seen each other at our annual Convocation, so she asked Edith, "Supposing Janet and I were sent together, how would we get on?" "You wouldn't," Edith apparently replied, "you both like your own way too much." I didn't think that Edith knew me that well but I suppose she saw us both as fairly strong characters. Elizabeth didn't know me at all but had seen me amongst a group of deaconesses and later told me that I seemed to be the life and soul of the party. That didn't impress her as she was far more reserved. I am a gregarious animal and love the cut and thrust of lively banter and the sharing of good conversation.

Well, she soon found out that I was indeed to be her colleague and I was invited to the caravan before Edith and Elizabeth left the area and before I left Staveley. Perhaps the thing I remember most about that visit is that, as we sat talking together, an animal that seemed to me like a large rat, bolted up the caravan. I was told, "That's Moses, Edith's guinea pig, but she can't take him with her to the training centre in Liverpool; we wondered if he might stay on the caravan". Well, what could I say? "Okay", I replied, "As long as you look after him". So there were to be three of us on the caravan the following year!

Elizabeth and I chatted together with our colleagueship in view. I asked what had been happening in their missions and was told about the starting of Young Wives' groups and various things that had evidently shown God at work. But I wanted to hear more of personal salvation and changed lives. Was it that we had different priorities or that we expressed ourselves differently? We were soon to find out. Suffice it to say that neither of us were impressed by the other and we wondered just how well we would work together. But our God is a God of surprises and if He has our obedience He can work miracles.

September 1964 saw us beginning a year of mission in the Liverpool District and our first port of call was the Isle of Man. Neither of us had been there before but the one thing I had heard about was the TT Races. I wondered if they would be taking place whilst we were there and began to get quite excited. However, I was later to discover that they took place in the summer. Our stay would be from September to December. But The Grand Prix races would be taking place as we arrived in September. So I was not to be deprived altogether.

We boarded the Manxman together and Elizabeth was not impressed to see me in full deaconess uniform – but it was the easiest way to carry it! Before we reached the Isle of Man she had heard my life story. At least, that's how it seemed to her. But, after all, we were to live and work together for a year, so the sooner we knew each other, the better. There were then four circuits of the island and we missioned in each one, beginning in the Ramsey circuit in Bride and Michael. This was in the north of the island and I think it came to be our favourite area, though there were many other lovely places. For our first mission the caravan was parked in Bride. And it was while we were there that we joined the crowds lining the route of The Grand Prix races and watched some spectacular driving. Usually, the caravan was our home but in the Isle of Man, while we could work in it, eat in it, hold meetings in it and generally use it as our base, the laws connected with the boarding house trade did not allow us to use it as a dwelling and so we could not sleep in it. I think special permission was given, however, for us to do this in subsequent missions. But at Bride we slept at the home of Mr. and Mrs. Skinner. He had a Riley 1.5, a lovely little car that it was my delight to drive, quite a contrast with my old Standard 8. They treated us as part of the family. We slept in a large bedroom in which there was a double and a single bed, I was in the double! But I was in for a surprise the following morning when Elizabeth rose at about six o'clock and came to get me out of bed, threatening to drip water out of the water bottle onto me if I didn't get up. In fact, she began to do just that and I didn't think it was funny, especially on someone else's bed. "Don't ever do that again," I told her. Yes, I was cross. She still had probationers' studies to do but I didn't. And being the person she was, she intended to have her studies completed before the rest of the day's work began. The incident was soon forgotten (temporarily!) and it was her turn to be on the receiving end when at the meal table later on I told her she reminded me of Hattie Jaques! She wasn't impressed until I said that Hattie Jaques had a lovely smile.

Those days in Bride were very happy days. Yes, we did have different priorities. I was always very keen that we should be well prepared for meetings, especially since for some people there it might be the only occasion when they would hear the gospel and perhaps even make a personal response. Elizabeth was equally insistent that we visit every house in the neighbourhood and meet people wherever we could, so both things we done thoroughly. Our differences were to contribute to a very good colleagueship and excellent team work. In fact, we were later to receive a letter from a retired missionary expressing her appreciation of the way in which God was using us as a team. This team-work was a great advantage as we met with young people in the caravan for the Friday evening youth squash. Elizabeth would leave me to welcome them while she prepared the drinks. As we settled down to discussion, encouraging them to talk and question, we became quite adept at throwing the ball back and forth so that the strengths of either one of us came into play.

There was already a group of young people at the Bride Chapel and they soon became very involved in the mission. We missioned in Michael at the same time and had some good contacts amongst the young people there. In fact, one of them, Rosemary, who was about sixteen years old, came over to Bride for some of the meetings. She gave us a very pleasant surprise one evening when she told us that she had made her personal commitment to Jesus during the mission. We had known nothing about it. Though we sometimes gave an opportunity for people to make their response public, perhaps by coming to the communion rail during the singing of a hymn or in some other way, we knew that this had not been the way for Rosemary. Hers had been a private commitment, simply a transaction between her and God, and how many others may have come this way too?

The Sunday School at Michael was very poorly attended but we had the usual full house at Sunshine Corner, the evening meeting for children. Some of the leaders wondered if that meeting might be continued after the mission and so we met with them to talk over methods and introduce them to new material and some came into the Sunshine Corner to observe. The result was that these meetings did continue and the hope was that the Sunday School would grow as a consequence. We certainly believed that some children could and would make a personal response to the gospel, though we never asked them to do this openly. Rather, we encouraged them to come and talk to us if they had any questions or wanted to ask Jesus into their lives. Some did, and those times of real commitment were often like a foretaste of heaven. In Bride we held meetings for children on three nights a week and the numbers grew to about fifty. On other evenings we met teenagers in the caravan and this proved especially fruitful. As we thought together of what it really means to be a Christian and of the cost of following Christ, a stirring of desire and not a little conflict went on in some hearts. We were thrilled when Graham who was almost fourteen years of age, came to us and said that he had been thinking deeply about these things and wanted to know more. That same evening, during the adult meeting, he made a public declaration of his acceptance of Christ. We knew that others wanted to do the same but lacked courage. Graham's 16- year-old sister, Joan, was one, and not until we had moved to Michael and she came to the mission there did she finally reach the end of the struggle. The point of submission to Christ came for her as we talked together in the caravan after the meeting.

In Michael we met a very interesting lady. It was obvious that she was a Christian and we asked her to share a word of testimony in one of the evening meetings. We were totally unprepared for the surprise as we listened to her story. A French lady, she had found her way to the Isle of Man by marrying a Manxman. However, during the second World War she had, as a teenager, been involved in very dangerous work. A Church of Scotland

Minister who became known as the Tartan Pimpernel spent his time in rescuing Jewish children from occupied France and she worked alongside him. She told of carrying messages in her shoes and narrowly escaping the Gestapo as they visited the house where she had been staying. Life was very uncertain, but she asserted that it was easier to be a Christian in that situation than in her present one because in those difficult times you were thrown completely upon God and depended upon Him absolutely. The Lord blessed us in the Ramsey circuit. For some people it was a time for new commitment and when we left they continued the morning prayer meeting at twenty to ten.

From there we moved to the Castletown circuit where we missioned in the village of Colby and in Croit-E-Caley, a neighbouring hamlet. In our general visiting we had some good conversations and in two house meetings some good discussion. The meetings on church premises were not too well supported and the Sunshine Corner meetings suffered through an epidemic of measles in the village. The most rewarding, yet frustrating aspect of the work here was that amongst the teenagers, most of whom came to the Youth Squashes in the caravan. Since leaving Sunday School they had had no contact with the church and there was no provision in the village for any kind of youth activities. There were some "tough" lads amongst these young people, but they were all ready and eager to talk about the Christian faith. We were invited to their gang hut and in return for our visit they came to the final Sunday service. It was heartbreaking to leave this group as "sheep without a shepherd".

The third mission was in the Douglas circuit where we missioned on the Willaston housing estate of about six hundred houses. More concentration was needed than we were able to give and we had to think of the best way of using the two weeks here. We asked for lists of lapsed members and parents of Sunday School scholars and on these we concentrated, though we met quite a bit of indifference. The young people on the estate could be quite "wild" but we soon won their confidence. There was no provision in the church for any youth activities during the week, apart from the Christian Endeavour which catered for the 11–14 age group and was hardly the thing for rough teenagers. On 5th November we had a wonderful response to the 'Bonfire and Barbecue' with some of the adults setting up the barbecue and doing the cooking while the teenagers helped in serving minerals. This widened our contacts, but by this time the mission was nearly over. One thing that did prove very worthwhile was the morning prayer meeting and on Wednesdays this was combined with coffee.

Elizabeth had the privilege of leading one woman of a rather anxious disposition to Christ during the course of an afternoon's visiting and a public witness was made at the evening meeting. A 16-year-old girl who had come to know Christ during the mission at Bride came over to give a word of testimony at one of the meetings. This was her first time of public witness and we were very thrilled to hear her. Though we didn't see much outward response to the gospel here we were aware of God's Spirit moving amongst us.

Before we moved from Bride I had been thinking about the old Standard 8 and wondering just what we should do if it gave up the ghost altogether. We had managed to purchase a new tyre to replace one that was almost bald but neither of us had a healthy bank balance – if we had one at all! Quite a number of people had been extolling the virtues of the Morris Minor 1000, but it seemed that a second-hand one was like gold to come by. What were we going to do, I asked Elizabeth. She told me she had just been reading a book by Hannah Hurnard who apparently, in her missionary work, needed some form of transport. She made this a matter of prayer and her prayers were wonderfully answered. "So," said Elizabeth, "we pray about it." And that is what we had been doing. As we talked to one or two people about the possibility of finding a second-hand Minor 1000 they were quite adamant that we should not find one anywhere on the island. After moving to Douglas I was having my prayer time one morning and as I read "Daily Light", a series of connected Scriptures for each day, one jumped out at me, the one from the letter of James, "Faith without works is dead." "Elizabeth," I said to her later, "we have to do something today." "What do you mean?" she asked. "We have been praying," I replied, "and we believe God will answer our prayers, but we have to do something. Faith without works is dead." I told her of my prayer time and the strong urge that I felt to take some action. "Well," she said, "what do you suggest we do?" "The obvious thing," I replied, "is to go to a garage and make some enquiries." So this we did. We called into the Athol garage in Douglas and spoke to the man in charge. "Do you have any second-hand Minor 1000s?" we asked. "Not at the moment," he replied, "but I have a fleet of them coming in later; they have been out on 'Hire and Drive'." "What sort of price would you be expecting for your Standard 8?" Having a fairly good idea that it might be worth fifty to sixty pounds, I replied, "A hundred pounds." "Right," he said, "come back later." I was amazed that he didn't even want to take it for a drive. Its condition was fairly obvious from the wear and tear on the bodywork. However, we did go back later and saw the very Minor 1000 that we felt was for us. I don't remember the price of it but we were allowed the hundred pounds on the Standard 8 and from somewhere we had to find another hundred or two. Prices were quite different then; you spoke in hundreds rather than thousands. Even so it was all quite daunting. Yet, with what we could scrape together plus a little help from family the cost was met and on 3rd December 1964 we drove away in a lovely Minor 1000, giving thanks to God for yet another miracle.

The final mission in the island saw us at St. John's in the Peel circuit. Here was Tynwald Hill where the official declarations of the Manx government are made. Right next to it was the lovely Anglican church, having its own royal seat and bishop's chair. Somewhat overshadowed, on the opposite side of the road, were the unimpressive buildings of the Methodist church. The Methodist society was small, but there was a good spirit there.

After visiting the school, where the headmaster was a Methodist, we had children from far and wide to the Sunshine Corner. The Youth Squashes were very worthwhile and it seemed to be to our advantage that the Anglican youth club that usually met on a Friday, had been closed down for a few weeks, owing to the misbehaviour of certain members. They were all very keen to talk and ask questions and though we saw no evidence of real commitment to Christ, we were aware that many were thinking deeply.

While the caravan remained sited at St. John's, we also missioned at Greeba, a much smaller village. Here, they still talked in glowing terms about the Caravan Mission they had had ten years previously when a number of teenagers had been converted. It was good to see them and their families, now faithful members of the church. Here the mission was really to the church, to encourage and strengthen, though we had, I think, all the children of the neighbourhood to Sunshine Corner. The final rally of the mission was also the final rally of the island Methodists we had met during our term there. This was held at St. John's and supported by the Peel Salvation Army band. One of the greatest thrills was to see some of the teenage boys from Colby there. They had made their own way there and not without much effort. Before we left Colby we had suggested that the floor be levelled in the ex-Primitive Methodist building across the road, now used for Sunday School, and that it be used for youth activities, with some leadership from a certain young school-teacher. Our suggestions were frowned upon, however, because the young school-teacher was not right in the life of the church, though we felt he might be drawn further in if encouraged, and he was certainly willing to help in this way. We left Colby rather disappointed about this, but later heard from the Chairman of the District that the suggestions had been accepted. Another miracle, for which we praise God!

Despite some disappointments, Caravan Mission work was very rewarding. It was not, however, a Summer holiday experience. We missioned through the year, come rain, hail or shine. We had the privilege of missioning in some lovely places and the joy of meeting some of God's saints. But there were also those occasions when huge icicles hung from the caravan and we had to be dug out of a few feet of snow. And it was no picnic to have to dig a deep enough hole where we could empty our Elsan toilet, especially in rough weather! The caravan was only eighteen feet by seven, nothing like today's sturdy mobile homes and it sometimes had to withstand powerful winds. It was while we were at St. John's on Tynwald Green that we had one of our fiercest gales. The caravan rocked and the water spilled out of the kettle spout. Elizabeth suggested that we were in for a cold night as we should not dare to leave the paraffin heater alight. When I expressed doubts about being without heating all night she said, "Well, take your pick, freeze to death or burn alive!" We survived the night and were still glad to be on mission work. I think it was on the following day that the circuit steward presented us with a poem he had written, which is as follows:

Rock-a-bye, sisters, in the Manx gale,
The caravan shudders, the hurricane wails.
A trip on the Manxman is surely the best
For giving the tummy a practical test,
But this will be nothing for those who have been
Rocked in a bunk upon Tynwald Green.

Even so, we wouldn't have chosen to miss our time in the Isle of Man.

After the Christmas break, a little longer than our usual three days, we returned to the Liverpool District, missioning in the villages of Tarleton and Rufford in the Ormskirk circuit. The caravan was sited in Tarleton for the first half of the mission and in Rufford for the second half so that both in turn had the advantage of the morning prayer group and the Friday Youth Squashes. Tarleton was a large village and Rufford not much smaller, so house-to-house visiting of the whole area was out of the question but we visited schools with good results and one of the public houses where we were well-received. The minister and people of Tarleton had made good preparations for this mission and the house parties enabled us to make contact with a good percentage of non-church-goers. The discussions were very worthwhile and in some places continued to a very late hour! In Rufford, on a small estate of about a hundred houses we had a house party attended by about seventeen people, only about four of whom had regular contact with the church. Some of them later came to a church service.

Tarleton, at this time, was a very active society with a morning congregation of sixty to seventy and an evening congregation of about forty to fifty. The

Sunday School was extremely well run and flourishing. Only one age group was not catered for in the weeknight activities and that was the younger children. Sunshine Corners were greatly appreciated and were continued after the mission. Five youngsters from this group came to see us and asked Christ into their lives.

When the caravan was moved on to Rufford and sited in the grounds of the church we soon found it attracting attention. Local teenagers came to investigate and from the interior of the caravan we listened to their colourful language! Then we emerged to greet them and introduce ourselves as well as explaining why we were there. "So what is there for us?" asked one of them. "The Youth Squash," we replied. "What's that?" they wanted to know. "You lot squashed into this caravan on Friday night," we retorted. And what a squash it was! They came and brought their friends. We juggled with cups of tea and beakers of squash, slotted in a brief prayer and had a great to and fro discussion. And they came again ... and again.

One evening a few in their late teens joined them, one of them with his powerful Norton motorcycle. I went out for a closer look. "Can I have a go?" I enquired. "Yes," he replied, "jump on the back". "No," I said, "I mean can I take it for a spin?" "Have you got a licence?" he wanted to know. "Yes," I replied and he duly handed over his bike. My colleague tells me that as I took off he remarked, "She can handle it better than I can". I can hardly believe that a tough young fellow would say that, even if he thought it, but he was certainly impressed. It was a great link between these young folk and ourselves. God certainly uses ordinary things for extraordinary purposes. And again, in that place He worked miracles. We knew that some of these young folk were being challenged by the gospel. They talked one day about the prayers they had in school, 'just read from a book' and then commented, "But you talk to God as if He were really there, as if you really know Him." "Well," we replied, "we do," and we were able to share our own story, our own experience of Jesus.

The climax came shortly before we left. Answering a knock on the caravan door, we saw some of the young teenagers. Billy was the spokesman. "We want to do, you know, what you said," he blurted out. "You mean," I replied, "you want to ask Jesus Christ into your life." "Yes," was the answer. We invited them into the caravan and we sat and talked about what real commitment meant. "I know we've been swearing a lot," said one of the boys, "but we want to ask Jesus to help us." As we led them to the point of handing over their lives to Christ as we prayed together, the presence of God was very real.

In counselling them afterwards about growing in the Christian life we pointed out that now Jesus was the boss (the term "Lord" might have signified very little to them) and the important thing was to do what He said in everything. It was certainly a very sincere commitment but there was no obvious leader to shepherd them in the next part of their journey. Some of the folk in the church seemed rather more concerned about keeping their premises intact than shepherding the lambs. We still pray for them, forty years on, that God will have His hand upon them.

Our time in the Southport Banks circuit was not as rewarding owing to lack of preparation. The Sunshine Corners, however, were very well attended and worthwhile. The Youth Squashes were so well attended that we had to move out of the caravan into a room in the new Sunday School building. One highlight for us was the visit of the boys who were converted at Rufford. Each Monday we entertained them to tea and they stayed on to the Youth Squashes. It was wonderful to see their continued interest and their changing attitudes.

The next mission was in the Southport North circuit in the village of Crossens. Here much prayer had been offered and everything well prepared. The people had been encouraged and informed by their minister, Rev. Ron Bradwell, another of God's saints. He was a man with a pastor's heart and an evangelist's zeal. The normal programme of church activities was not suspended, but re-arranged so that all could be incorporated into the mission programme. So we were able to go into Cadets, Life Boys, Girls' Life Brigade, Sunday School, Women's Meeting and Wives' Fellowship throughout the campaign, whilst taking Sunshine Corners and other meetings. This meant constant contact with all age groups. The house parties presented invaluable opportunities of contact with people outside the church and the meetings on church premises were extremely well-attended. Eleven young people accepted Jesus into their lives and it was good to be able to give them Bible reading notes and talk with them about living the Christian life. There were some good Sunday School teachers who shared these joys with us and would be able to shepherd these youngsters.

The teenagers who came to the Youth Squashes on Sunday and Friday evenings were rather more intellectual than some we had had so we had to be on our toes. It was good to know that when we left, the Sunday Youth Squash was to be continued in various homes. Some of these young people took part in the annual procession of witness organised by the Southport Council of Churches and it was a great delight to us to see the boys from Rufford in this procession, looking so smart and unashamed to own their Lord. At the final rally of the mission the minister invited people to say what the mission had meant to them. Some did, and some talked afterwards about the way they had been blessed. The gospel was talked up in the streets, especially by the children, and the effects of this mission were felt in the community.

It was while we were here in the areas of Tarleton and Crossens that we met three couples who were to become life-long friends. George was the head of the secondary school in Tarleton and his wife, Jean, was a wonderful hostess and very skilled in flower-arranging and other crafts. Jean nursed us both through gastric flu and their home was a wonderful refuge. Before we left, they gave us the key of the door to their house. And that spoke volumes. We have seen their two boys grow up and marry and have never lost touch. Ann and Bruce were another couple whose support and hospitality we valued so much. Ann was in teaching and Bruce in market gardening until the bottom almost fell out of the market. But the taste of those lettuces and tomatoes as well as potatoes, cauliflowers and other vegetables has yet to be surpassed. Jean and Jack were in Crossens and very active in the church. Jack was an electrician and for this and countless other reasons was always in great demand. Their two children, Sue and David, are now well-married, but we remember walking into their house as Jean was walking out to be taken to hospital for David's delivery into this world. Some time later I baptised him. I can hardly believe that the now six foot well-built fellow is the same person! The tapestry of our lives has been greatly enhanced through knowing these three wonderful couples.

We moved from the Southport area to the Skelmersdale circuit, working from the Digmoor and Upholland churches. Much demolition work was being done and new buildings erected to cope with the overspill population of Liverpool, so the landscape was rapidly changing. We felt that four months would have been more desirable and profitable than the four weeks we had here. While we visited in both Digmoor and Upholland all the meetings on church premises were held at Digmoor; there were only about two and a half miles between them. The meetings were well-attended with a lot of circuit support. In one of these meetings Joan, a 17-year-old girl, made a public response to Christ. Though already a Christian she was challenged by Romans, chapter ten and verse nine: "if you confess with your lips that Jesus is Lord and believe in your heart that God raised Him from the dead, you will be saved." She had believed in her heart but felt she needed to confess this publicly. She very much wanted to be a nurse and felt a call to the mission field. Soon her training began and she did, in fact, spend a good number of years on the mission field.

The house parties gave an opportunity of contact with people outside the church. People came and talked freely and the conversations were in no way superficial. The people of the two churches decided to continue the house parties as newcomers moved into the area. Three Sunshine Corners a week were held at Digmoor and these were well attended, but we were concerned that those on the estate in Upholland were missing out. Concern about this was also expressed by one of the members who offered her home as a meeting place. So we arranged an extra Sunshine Corner and the children flocked to the house. When numbers reached eighty-five one week we wondered just how we could accommodate any more. The members of the church decided to continue this meeting, especially with a view to the integration of the young people into the Sunday School of the coming new church. Their hope was to hire the Civil Defence hall so that no children need be turned away.

The people on the estate were also keen that a prayer meeting should take place there too, so the Wednesday twenty-to-ten prayer meeting was held in one of the homes with about twenty people attending regularly. One lady who lived across the road and who had no church connections asked if she could come and she came each week, attending other meetings too. It was planned to continue the prayer meeting when the mission was over. The people had been greatly blessed through this time together and God's presence was very real.

The Youth Squashes, too, were so well supported and such a blessing that plans were made for these to continue after the mission in various homes after the Sunday evening service. God's Spirit was certainly at work amongst us during this mission.

Our next move was to the Earlstown and Lowton circuit where we missioned in the areas of the Lowton Road and Lane Head churches. It says much for the enthusiasm and concern of the church at Lowton Road that two representatives visited us during our stay in the Skelmersdale circuit, wanting to know how they could prepare for the forthcoming mission. The mission proved to be one of great blessing as there were those who longed to reach out to others in Christ's Name. The caravan was parked outside the Lowton Road church and those who were able came to the twenty to ten prayer meeting. A prayer meeting was also called after one of the Sunday services, especially to pray for the mission.

The children came in crowds to the Sunshine Corner and three girls of Junior school age came to see us and asked Jesus into their lives. There was a lot of questioning and heart searching in the Youth Squashes. "Does commitment to Christ mean keeping certain rules? Does it mean becoming a deaconess?" These and many other questions were asked and answered. The young people were also very much in evidence at other meetings during the mission.

Lane Head was a smaller society but there were a few people keen to reach out. Two of them came visiting with us with a view to inviting folk to a house party at their home. This and other house parties in the area went extremely well. We met people with little church contact and had some good discussions. One of the leaders of the society was keen for us to meet his two sons who, at sixteen and seventeen years of age, seemed to be drifting away from the church. We met them on the first Sunday, discovered they played guitars and asked them if they would help in some of the meetings. They were only too thrilled to be asked. I joined them with the trumpet and, alternatively, accompanied them on the piano and soon we had our own group! We even wrote our own song when we couldn't find one to fit the theme of one of the meetings. Our hope and prayer was, of course, that they would find their way into the Kingdom. Very few young people from Lane Head came to the Youth Squashes at Lowton Road. One girl, however, came to these and other meetings. After the final rally she approached us in tears; she had wanted to make a public response to Christ as others had, but had lacked the courage. However, her response had been made and we were able to counsel her. That final rally was a wonderful climax to the mission and a new beginning in a number of lives.

The last mission in the District was at Neston and Little Neston in the Bebington circuit where we spent three weeks, with the caravan sited in Little Neston. Both villages were small but in both churches there were plans for new building schemes in the hope of serving an expanding population. Our visiting was mainly of people with some church contact but we were able to borrow the Labour Party loud speaker and use it in Little Neston. Through this and the house parties we made contact with non-church-goers and had some lively and profitable discussions. The Youth Squashes were, as ever, very worthwhile. These were initially attended by church youngsters but on the last Friday a crowd of fairly rough teenagers gathered around the caravan and, with some persuasion, came in. They then attended the Sunday evening service as they had promised they would, much to the surprise of the church youngsters. They brought a number of their friends to the Youth Squash afterwards and we had the kind of Squash we were used to! Sadly the mission was ending as their interest was being quickened but the youth club leader, a capable and committed person, had plans to continue the Youth Squashes after the mission was over. The Sunshine Corners were well attended as usual and, with school holidays beginning before the mission ended, we were able to meet the children for games and a picnic tea one afternoon. Then we had a combined meeting for the children of the two villages. A number of them enquired about following Jesus and we were thrilled that some took the step of commitment to Him.

The meetings of the mission were well supported by the two churches and the circuit and had quite an impact on a number of church people. The final Sunday service was a combined service held at Neston. During the service a teenager from another part of the circuit made a public response to Christ and on the following evening, after the final rally, her sister came to talk with us and made her response too. This was a thrilling climax to a year so richly blessed by God.

3. The prize icicle of a winter mission

4. Janet and her B.S.A. 250 cc, having arrived for the first Caravan Mission in the Clitheroe circuit

5. Janet and Olive on Caravan “Joy”

6. Sailing to the Isle of Man. Janet with guinea pig

7. Janet and Elizabeth – trumpet practice in the caravan

8. Elizabeth, Eileen and Janet with
the minister in the Blackburn Circuit.

9. Staveley young people with their leader and Sister Janet

10. Ordination 1963
Sister Janet seated extreme right

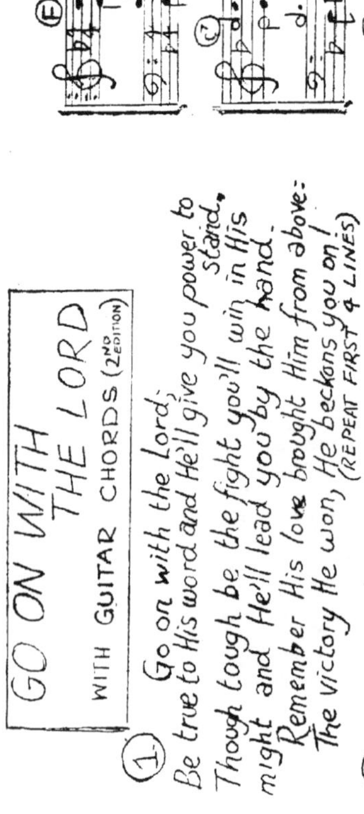

GO ON WITH THE LORD

WITH GUITAR CHORDS (2ND EDITION)

1. Go on with the Lord;
Be true to His word and He'll give you power to stand,
Though tough be the fight you'll win in His might and He'll lead you by the hand.
Remember His love brought Him from above;
The victory He won, He beckons you on!
(REPEAT FIRST 4 LINES)

2. His wisdom has planned your pathway and mine, and black as the night may be,
He's there by your side, your Friend and your Guide,
Both now and eternally;
Though doubts should assail, don't let them prevail,
One day you'll see why those clouds crossed your sky
(REPEAT FIRST 4 LINES)

Every penny will help to erect a New Building for Youth Work in the Service of Christ.

1/-

GO ON WITH THE LORD

SISTER JANET EDWARDS

F Bb F C7 F Bb F C7 F Bb F FINE C7 G C7 F D.C.

PUBLISHED BY THE NEW BUILDING FUND COMMITTEE OF MOUNT TABOR METHODIST CHURCH, NEW BRIMINGTON, CHESTERFIELD

11. Sister Janet's song published by the Staveley Young people.

Six

Miracles in Melton Mowbray

Another year of evangelistic work had come to a close but my hope was that a similar appointment would follow. I think the Warden of the Order knew this and did his best to bring it about but it was not to be. Elizabeth Hodgkiss, with whom I had shared a very happy year, was to go on caravan with Eileen Wright and the other caravans were fully staffed. So I had a year without appointment and went back to live at home and do some teaching. I was soon on the staff of a school in Swadlincote and settled in well. There was a happy atmosphere in the school and we had a very supportive head. My time there was even more fulfilling than I had expected; there was a good deal of interest in Christian things and before I left eighteen children had come to ask about beginning the Christian life and made their own personal commitment.

Elizabeth and Eileen were working in Yorkshire on the caravan and this was not too far for me to travel and take part in some of the meetings, especially the Youth Squashes at the weekend. On one visit Eileen posed the question, quite seriously, "Why don't you come and join us?" Well, I hadn't expected that, especially as I was Elizabeth's former colleague, though all three of us got on extremely well together. But to join them unofficially and, of course, without pay, would mean that we all had to be very sure that it was right. It was during my second term at school that I woke up one morning feeling very strongly that I should be on caravan mission work, but I needed a very definite sign from God that I should resign my post. I remember asking that He would send me five pounds! Not long afterwards gran put a five-pound note in my hand, but because I knew where that was from I asked for a further sign. When I approached the head to inform her of my intentions she was not happy at the prospect and was quite sure they would find no-one to replace me for the last term of the year. I told her that I was praying that they would and this, for me, would confirm the rightness of my decision. Well, in fact, they did, which rather surprised her and pleased me. So I joined Eileen and Elizabeth for the rest of that year and we had a wonderful and fruitful time together. Incidentally, the financial return from two terms' teaching was at least equal to the pay I should have received for a full year on caravan.

Caravan mission work by this time was being slowly phased out. Even though there were other pressing needs, such as the work in new housing areas, and money had to be diverted into this work, many of us felt that the work of caravan missions was still effective and worthwhile.

So where next? It was back into circuit to work with a minister we had met during our mission in Crossens. Rev. Ron Bradwell was moving to become superintendent minister of the Melton Mowbray circuit and asked if I could be appointed there. Knowing something of his priorities I felt sure that we should work well together. So in September 1966 I moved to Melton Mowbray in Leicestershire, the home of Stilton cheese and pork pies. At first I was in digs but then the circuit purchased a small, terraced house that was to become my home. I was to share the work in the main church with Ron and also have oversight of other churches. The people in Melton had not been used to a woman conducting worship, and preaching, and I think some of them were at first a little apprehensive. But they soon accepted me as a co-worker with Ron. In the village chapels for which I had responsibility there was no problem. In fact, I well remember the steward, another woman, taking me round the village of Somerby to meet the members and introducing me with the words, "This is our new minister."

As well as the main church in the town there was a church on a new housing estate, the Sandy Lane church. Soon after my arrival in Melton I went to speak at the Young Wives' fellowship there. I remember I spoke on "Who Jesus was and who Jesus is". I doubt that I would remember the theme of my addresses to many other fellowships but I guess this one was rather special. After the meeting a young woman came to talk to me. "My husband and I have recently become members of the church," she said, "but I didn't realise there was anything personal as you have spoken of it this afternoon. Could I come and talk to you?" Well, it was sad, of course, that people could have been received into membership without being given an opportunity to make a personal commitment to

Jesus and without being told that this was the first step into church membership. Nevertheless, it was wonderful that here was someone whose heart had been touched by God's Spirit and was so open to receive what He had to give. Val and I very soon met together and we talked about personal salvation, about Jesus, about commitment. I seem to remember leaving her with Revelation, chapter 3, verse 20, the words of Jesus, "Behold, I stand at the door and knock; if anyone hears my voice and opens the door, I will come in". She went away to ponder this and we agreed to meet again soon. It was, in fact, very soon that the phone rang one day and it was Val. "It's happened," she said. "I couldn't wait until I saw you again." Val had made her personal commitment and was experiencing a wonderful sense of God's presence and the joy of His salvation. It was great to meet again and rejoice together. Very soon others were noticing the difference. One of them was a neighbour who, apparently, commented to Val that her attitude to provocation was different: she was no longer swearing at the milkman! Val didn't at first grasp the opportunity to explain why but then made sure that she found an appropriate time to let her neighbour know what had happened. Becoming a Christian is not a private affair, personal, yes, as we enter into a meaningful relationship with Jesus, but private, no; our faith is to be shared. Val's husband, Geoff, a lovely, quiet man, didn't need to be told that something momentous had happened. Indeed, to him it seemed that there was another love in Val's life as, indeed, there was, though not one to lessen her love for him, but rather, to strengthen it. Val's great yearning now was for Geoff to discover this same love. So we began to pray that Geoff, too, would make his personal commitment to Jesus.

I was in Melton for three years. Exactly one year later, I received a letter from Geoff, dated 10th August 1970, which I still have. Val and I had kept in touch, of course, but here was a letter of good news! Geoff had asked Jesus into his life as Saviour. Though he was challenged after Val had become a Christian, the actual climax came through a Holiday Club at their church when three young people stayed in their home. Val, he said, was walking on air and I was so thrilled that God had answered prayer. It has been one of the greatest privileges of my life to point others to Jesus but God has so many ways into people's hearts and we are only ever links in a chain. But how wonderful it is to witness the working of God's Spirit in the lives of others.

Ron Bradwell was eager to see others embrace the faith and grow in grace and so a mission was planned at Whissendine, one of the village chapels in the Melton circuit. This we conducted ourselves and, having responsibility for the Whissendine society, I was privileged to have quite an input. There were those for whom this was a time of re-dedication and others who were challenged to take that first step of commitment to Christ. I have a letter now written by two rather shy teenage girls and headed, "How our life with Jesus began." It is another of my treasured possessions and I hope and pray that Janice and Doreen have stayed the course and grown in their Christian faith.

The routine work of visiting, preaching and numerous meetings went on, of course, and brought its own rewards and challenges, but I was still keen to do the work of an evangelist. Knowing this, some of the members at Great Dalby, in another section of the circuit, asked me if I would go into their young people's meeting for a number of weeks to talk to them about the Christian life and its implications for the individual. We had some good meetings and I know that this was backed up by prayer from the Great Dalby people. The result was that ten of those young people made their own commitment to Jesus. One of them, Irene, married one of the ministers in the circuit and it has been a great joy to meet them again recently and to know that forty years on they are still serving the Lord.

Somerby was a warm fellowship and I enjoyed having pastoral oversight there. Olive was a steward and young people's leader and a faithful worker. I had been into the young people's fellowship for which Olive had responsibility and, shortly before I left, she asked if I would do a series of mid-week meetings for them and present the challenge of personal commitment to Jesus. This I was very happy to do and the result was that ten young people committed their lives to Christ. During this time in Melton I was praying about the next move and feeling that God would make His way plain. I met with a leader of The Evangelisation Society but felt that their approach was too rigid and wasn't for me.

Elizabeth, after one year on caravan with Eileen, was given a year out of an appointment to finish her degree, during which time she taught in the mornings and studied the rest of the day. She sometimes came over to see me and to visit our friend, Jean, at Crossens. Toward the end of that year she heard where her next appointment would be. “Guess where I am going”, she said to me. I couldn’t, and when she said “Shetland”, I replied, “That’ll slow you down!” But, of course, I was wrong. Though a townie, born in Salford, she settled in Shetland and, after some initial setbacks, loved the place and the people. She went up the following September to a manse that had been empty for a year and was wet rather than damp. She had taken a black Labrador with her but after he chased a sheep into the voe (the sea inlet) he had to be destroyed. So when she first phoned me she said, “I don’t think I can stay here.” Sitting by the gas fire in my cosy little sitting room, I replied, “You will; we preach the grace of God and we have to live it!” She was also poorly with enteritis but the Shetlanders were wonderful and kept an eye on her. A car was provided for her use but she hadn’t passed her test. However, a young man travelled with her to her appointments, possibly hearing her sermons three or four times over. After saying she couldn’t stay, one of her readings, from “Daily Light” I think, included the words of Naomi to Ruth, “Wait, my daughter, until you learn how the matter turns out” or, in the Authorised Version, “Sit still, my daughter ...” (Ruth 3, verse 18). This was a clear word from God to her and she was obedient.

During the Christmas break I went up to see her and it was a pretty severe winter. It snowed and it was bleak and the roads icy. The manse, a small croft house on the hill, only about fifty yards from the Gruting chapel, was clothed in a white blanket. Sunday came when she was due to take a service in the chapel. We didn't think anyone would come, but Elizabeth was insistent that we make our way down to the chapel, which we did with great difficulty. The door was shut fast with the snow and ice but somehow we managed to open it. Of course, as we expected, there was no congregation, so we toiled back up the hill and on arrival at the manse I peeled the frozen snow off my fishnet tights. These soothmoothers, as the people from south of Shetland were called, had a lot to learn. I think I dressed more appropriately after that. After a few days I was aware of a very sore patch on my leg that felt rather like a boil. When I arrived back in Melton and saw the doctor, he said, "Wherever have you been to get this?" It was frostbite! But I recovered. It didn't deter me from going up again in the summer. We were able to get about and meet some of the people, take photographs and discover more of the beauty of Shetland. And I fell in love with the place. When I returned to Melton Shetland filled my thoughts. As I was driving around the circuit I had to stop the car and transfer my thoughts to paper. The following is what I wrote:

Dear Shetland Isle

Where is the vision that I saw
Of the hills and the sea on a far off shore?
Where is the splendour and the space
Of that beloved, rugged place
That rises from the northern sea,
A place so lately dear to me?

Four days ago I left behind
Folk of the gentlest, rarest kind,
Four days ago I came away,
Yet wished with all my heart to stay.
Four days ago! And yet it seems
As though I'd been there in my dreams.
The wonder lingers still with me,
But oh for the reality!

The trees are here but they hide the sky;
The folk are here but they all pass by,
And life is lived at such a pace
That one gets caught up in the race.
The roads are wide and we travel fast
And the last are first and the first are last
And there's always so much to be done
That our fervour dies with the setting sun.
We've lost the sense of being still
And waiting on a higher will;
We've lost the sense of being one
With all that lives beneath the sun;
We've lost the sense of being – just
The sense of being God's rich dust.

Oh when shall I return to thee,
My rock, surrounded by the sea,
Dear Shetland Isle? I long to come
And live my life and feel at home.
I want to lie and gaze and gaze
On the hills where the sheep so quietly graze.
I want to look up to the great arched sky
And watch the seagull soaring high.
I want to step out over hills of peat
And feel the turf beneath my feet,

To travel the moor where the ponies roam
And all the wild creatures are so much at home,
And then to return to the house on the hill,
At peace with the world and content in God's will.

Janet I Edwards

In God's will was where I wanted to be and so I awaited the news of my stationing for the following year. It was quite different from the norm. In fact, the Warden of the Order and two of his colleagues came to see me. He was well aware of my preference for evangelistic work and also aware that I was thinking about getting some of the songs I had written into print as a number of people had asked for them. They were gospel songs for the guitar. So we met together and talked. Then came his proposal. "You've been to visit Elizabeth in Shetland and know something of the situation. How would you feel about going there to take the place of a minister who is having to retire early through ill health and keeping yourself? You would live at Scalloway in the neighbouring circuit to Elizabeth's and the appointment would be for one year. The hope is that another minister will be stationed there in the following year. You might also do something about getting your songs into print." Well, this I hadn't expected and it did seem a pretty tall order. But the prospect of going to Shetland was wonderful. I didn't have to think long before giving him my answer in the affirmative.

Goodbyes were said, but not only to the people in the churches. During my time in Melton I had joined the town band, playing first cornet. I think our practice night was Tuesday so this became officially my day off. I had enjoyed playing with the band, especially at local events such as garden parties and sports days. On my last occasion with them they presented me with a brown leather document case that I still have and use. It is one of my treasures.

In Melton I had a small garden and I have always loved gardening. Knowing this, one of the men from the circuit came up with what seemed a good idea. “What you need up there, my gel, is a few hens,” he suggested. He was a farmer and had a prize strain of Rhode Island Reds. Furthermore, he offered to crate up half a dozen pullets and a cock so that I could take them with me. So, when my time in Melton came to an end I left with this crate of pullets, travelling first to my parents’ home for a short break before driving up to Aberdeen to board the boat for Shetland.

Seven

Shetland Bound

Taking hens to Shetland was all very well, but I was to be based in Scalloway and the manse was a flat. One of the first things, therefore, was to phone Elizabeth who was out in the country, about the prospect of acquiring a hen house. "Elizabeth," I said, "I'm bringing up a crate of hens or, to be precise, six pullets and a cock. Can you get a hen house in place?" "Yes," she replied, "I'm sure I can do that and there is space here for a run, but you will look after them!" Well, that could be sorted; the chief thing was to have a home for the hens when we arrived. My next phone call was to the deaconess living in Edinburgh, asking about the possibility of breaking my journey there and travelling on to Aberdeen the next day. "Well, actually I shall be away," she said, "but don't worry, I'm sure I can get you fixed up with one of our members." The next thing was to break the news about the hens. "No problem," she said, "I'm sure Mary, who was at one time a land girl in Cumbria, will be only too pleased to accommodate you and the hens as well." And Mary was.

So with luggage, hens and their food and drink, we set off for Edinburgh. At appropriate times I stopped to feed and water the stock as well as for my own refreshment. I was already beginning to look on them as my family and it brought back memories of my childhood days when gran and grandad kept hens. On arrival in Edinburgh I did my best to follow the directions I had been given to the house where Mary lived. Imagine my surprise when I discovered that she had a flat on the third storey! I went to the door and was soon greeted by her grown-up son, Peter, and introduced to Mary. "You know I have a crate of hens," I volunteered. "Yes," said Mary, "Peter will bring them up." So hens, luggage and all were brought into the flat where one room had been specially prepared by Mary. Boxes with brush stales lying across them were evidently for perching. I was quite surprised that she intended to give them their freedom for a night, but I assured her that, being pullets, they were not yet ready for perching. So we left them to their new-found freedom. Mary made me very welcome and I enjoyed her hospitality. She worked at the hospital so next morning was up early and off, leaving Peter and me to finish breakfast and get sorted. So, then to see how my little family was. Well, what a sight and what a smell! What more could you expect? But someone had to clear up the mess and the only place to dispose of things was down the toilet. Peter directed operations. Plenty of newspaper and then plenty of soap and water was the order of the day. Eventually the hens were crated up again and taken to the boot of my car. So we set off for Aberdeen. There we boarded the Shetland boat for the 13-hour overnight journey. I watched the car being hoisted aloft before being set down in its place in the hold. This was before the days of the roll-on, roll-off ferries. Then I found my cabin and soon was settled for the night. It wasn't too choppy but I deemed it wise to stay put until morning.

It was light as the boat pulled into the harbour in Lerwick, Shetland's capital. Just a small town, there was plenty of hustle and bustle as boats arrived or left. Elizabeth was there to meet me and I think our first port of call was the Chairman's house in Lerwick. Harry and Ella Fosse usually provided breakfast for Methodists arriving by the early boat. Then we were on our way to Scalloway with some of my luggage and thence to Gruting to settle in the hens at Elizabeth's manse. This was a lovely run over to the West side of Shetland. Undulating countryside and a notable absence of trees and the sea never far away meant frequent panoramic views; the beauty was breathtaking. There was only one place in Shetland, perhaps more sheltered than others, where trees could be found and that was a mere copse of caricatures. Wherever you were, the sea was never more than three miles away. This was crofting country and the sheep and ponies roamed freely across the countryside. There seemed to be such a peace about the place.

After the forty minute drive we arrived in Gruting, an area of scattered crofts and here I was at home again, looking across the voe where there could be such spectacular sunsets. I don't think any other Methodist manse could have a view to equal it, let alone surpass it. There, sure enough, was the hen-house, with ground pegs driven in on either side and the toughest wire stretched between them over the top of the hen-house to anchor it against the driving winds. There was also a good-sized run between the manse and the outside wall which surrounded the garden area about four to five yards away. Wire netting also ran along the top of this wall lest any little pullet felt like taking off! The garden, of course, would need fencing off, but we would get to that when I had dug over the turf and created the garden. So the hens were installed. Nesting boxes and perches were all in order in the hen house and the floor covered in peat dust that was more freely available in Shetland than straw or hay.

Thus began an exciting adventure. The hens, of course, were my responsibility as Elizabeth had made clear, but I had my work to do in the Lerwick and North Isles circuit and, in addition, I was hoping to do some teaching so that I had something to live on. The next thing would be to apply for a job. In fact, I had already been in touch with the Education Authority before coming to Scalloway and I had an interview coming up. They knew I had been trained for Primary School education and that music was my main subject and the trumpet my main instrument. All went well and I was left to choose between general teaching and peripatetic music with some brass teaching in Lerwick High School. I opted for peripatetic music and brass teaching. What a gift, to travel the island teaching music, learning more about the wonderful wild-life and using my camera to capture it.

In the main the schools to which I travelled were small country schools and most of them, but not all, Primary schools. They had been without a music teacher for some time and I was told by more than one head teacher, "These bairns canna sing." Of course I didn't believe that they couldn't sing and my reply was, "If you didn't use your arms for some time you would probably lose the use of them or have to work very hard to recover the use of them." So I assured the head teachers that the bairns would sing again! I think I had some very pleasantly surprised head teachers when the Christmas concerts came round. Of course, as well as singing, we listened to music and learned to appreciate it and we made music, especially with tuned and untuned percussion instruments.

In the Secondary schools things were a little different. Most of the older boys would have written music out of their curriculum and definitely did not sing, except on one occasion, and that was during Up Helly Aa, the annual re-enactment of a Viking funeral when a replica Viking ship was burned after being paraded through the streets of Lerwick. This festival is a reminder of days long gone when the Vikings, at the end of the winter solstice, came in their longships across unchartered wastes of sea, raiding and plundering. During the dark winter days, men and boys in Lerwick work on building the Viking longship with its beautifully carved dragon's head and tail. The oars, surmounted by shields bearing heraldic emblems, are positioned on the gunwales and the raven banner of the Norsemen flies aloft. It is a thirty feet long masterpiece. As the great day of celebration dawns it is there on the quayside, on view for all to see. In the evening the Guizer Jarl and his squad lead the procession as the ship is paraded through the streets of Lerwick. The brass band strikes up with the Up Helly Aa songs and the men and boys sing lustily. Finally they fling their lighted torches into the ship and watch it burn. Amazingly, hardly any accidents happen during this festival. The celebrations continue far into the night as people gather in various halls. But why then did the male population feel that singing was not for them, except on this one occasion? It happened even in some of our churches where you could have a whole row of men holding their hymn books but not singing a word. We never did really find a satisfactory answer to this phenomenon. However, it was my job to teach music and to make it attractive to the young people.

There were really very few, if any, discipline problems in the schools but one school to which I was assigned presented a few challenges. This was the secondary school in Scalloway. I think the previous peripatetic music teacher had had a bit of a rough ride, so I went in prepared to meet things head on! Some of the lads were taller than I was but I let them know who was in charge. There was a definite antipathy to music and especially to singing so I devised some schemes of work, such as ‘Music through the ages’, which I hoped would create some interest. I also made use of tuned and untuned percussion so that while I played the piano they could provide the accompaniment. I think some of them came to enjoy striking three chime bars simultaneously to make a chord and coming in at the appropriate time as I played ‘Grandfather’s clock’ and similar tunes. Yes, we made some progress and I think maybe for some of them music moved some way up the agenda. It was interesting that this was the school visited by a music inspector who seemed to be impressed by what was happening. I had a good report. He evidently knew that I was a deaconess and I discovered that he was the organist of Wesley's Chapel in London. He invited me back to his hotel for tea and we had a good conversation, some of it concerning the gospel songs I had written. "Let it be the artist in you that comes through," he said, and I found his constructive criticism very helpful.

The brass teaching was mainly in the Lerwick High School where I taught trumpet and trombone, but I was soon asked to do some class teaching and some aural work with individuals who were working towards A-Level exams. I have to say I enjoyed the work in Primary schools much more. One of the schools I visited regularly was the Gruting Primary school which had just nine pupils. The head teacher, Mary Sutherland and her husband, Andy, were active members of the Methodist church, so we had quite a lot to do with them. Mary was an excellent teacher and loved her pupils. I remember they did a scheme of work about the countryside and one day we took the pupils down to the voe, sat in a boat and sang songs with the guitar. The school was used for social occasions too and one regular activity was an eight-o'clocks evening, when most of the community would be present. A good number contributed to the programme as most of the entertainment in these scattered communities had to be a D.I.Y. job. So readings, recitations, especially of Shetland poetry, sketches and the like were all enjoyed. Of course, some music was expected from me but I was keen to involve others. I was still playing the piano-accordion as well as the guitar and piano so was able to ring the changes. The ladies' knitting guild met in Gruting manse and I suggested that they might sing. "We canna sing," said one of them. "Can you shout Yoo-hoo?" I asked, pitching the notes for 'Yoo-hoo' as soh me, the fifth and third notes of the major scale. "Yeah," was the reply. "Then you can sing twa notes," I said. That was the beginning of a little group and we sang at the eight o'clocks.

I suppose I spent more nights at the Gruting manse than I did at the Scalloway manse so I was often able to give the hens their morning feed. When it was possible and tied in with my job I could give them the early evening feed. They were fed on meal in the morning mixed to a mash with any juicy tit-bits and corn in the afternoon. The ponies also knew when the red bowl of corn came out and they were soon gathered around asking for a taste. In the winter the mornings were dark, so much so that the children didn't start school until 9.30 a.m. There were not many hours of good daylight as it was getting dark again by around 3.00 p.m. So I had to be early enough in the afternoon to feed the hens before they went to their perches.

Soon I had a garden to fence off. Heavy digging was no problem in those days; in fact, I enjoyed it. There was no space for a garden at Scalloway, so I made the most of what there was at Gruting and also made myself a couple of cold-frames, using old windows. We did leave some of the turf to serve as a lawn and this gave us a bit of hay in the summer. Summer days in Shetland were wonderful. As the sun dipped over the horizon at midsummer it was only minutes before it rose again so there was hardly any darkness. You could have read a newspaper outside at midnight. The temptation was to work on outside until very late. One year I turned up a large strip of turf to extend the garden further and grew one hundred and three drum-head cabbages. We were able to feed the neighbourhood! It was never as hot as an English summer there, though even these seem to be changing. More often than not there would be a breeze and you might need a cardigan. Then as the months passed the winds seemed to increase. For this reason it was no use trying to grow runner beans or any tall plants. But we had some really good carrots, cabbages and swedes, or neeps, as they were called.

But there was work to be done inside the Gruting manse that presented a challenge. What had been a wash-house across the passageway from the kitchen served as a bathroom. The bath stood proudly on its feet, inviting those who dared to cross the passageway and take the plunge. There was no central heating but plenty of ventilation as the passageway led straight to the back door. I had brought with me the wood to box in the bath, having previously taken measurements, and so this was one of my first jobs. Then I began the decoration of the bathroom. It was while I was thus engaged that Kate put her head round the door. Seeing that I was trying to make improvements she asked, "Would you like twa or three tiles for the ceiling?" by which she meant enough to cover it.

Kate had been a lapsed Methodist member, but after visits from Elizabeth she came to the knitting guild, so called because during the whole of the meeting, except the prayer time, the ladies knitted. Time was very precious and this was part of their livelihood. They did it almost automatically so were able to give their attention to other things too. Then at the end of the meeting came the eats. The ladies themselves baked but their speciality was plain cooking and they made wonderful bannocks (no yeast), scones etc. So Elizabeth treated them to slightly richer fare, always baking at least five different things. The ladies did justice to her cakes!

Kate and her husband, Loll (Laurence), were joint owners, with his brother, of a furniture store in Lerwick and led very busy lives. Despite their comparative affluence they were totally unspoiled and very generous. I remember Kate speaking of one of their Christmases when she was a child. I think this was at one of the guild meetings when we were sharing memories of bygone Christmases. Kate told of one of the highlights of their Christmas and this was the sharing of an orange. She would get two segments but if a visitor called she might get only one. Kate became gradually more involved in the life of the church and I think it impressed her to see that we were workers, both inside the manse and outside. The manse comprised sitting-room, study, kitchen and one bedroom. When I decorated the sitting-room Kate was there again and we even had new carpet! But over a period the ladies' guild grew from about six or seven to around thirty. So we had the wall between sitting-room and study knocked down to make one big room.

The Scalloway manse was quite comfortable. In due course my two items of furniture, a radiogram and a record cabinet, arrived by boat, but other furnishings and fittings belonged to the manse. The church was in the same complex so I didn't have far to travel for the Scalloway services, though some preaching appointments meant a journey by boat The most northerly appointments were to Unst and Yell but I usually managed to get back the same day. Another church where I preached occasionally was on Burra Isle, not far as the crow flies but again, another boat journey. In fact, there was a small room in the church where there was a bed just in case the preacher had to stay overnight. This depended, of course, on whether it was fit to journey by the small boat. Since then a bridge has been built across to Burra Isle so no more boat journeys.

The Lerwick and North Isles circuit, of which Scalloway was a part, was long and narrow, stretching from Unst in the north to Fair Isle in the south, a distance of about sixty miles, so there was considerable travelling between the fourteen churches. The Shetland mainland was only about fifty miles in length and at its widest point no more than twenty miles across, but there were still many single track roads. The Walls circuit, which included Gruting, was a mere bulge on the west side of the mainland, about nine to ten miles from west to east and about the same in length. But, again, there were many single-track roads and the crofts were scattered over the hills. Much of Elizabeth's pastoral work was therefore done on foot, and this not only to Methodist members of her eight churches but to every household in the neighbourhood.

Methodism was very much alive in Shetland and its history goes back to the eighteen hundreds and begins with a man called John Nicholson. A Shetlander, he left the island in his teens, enlisted in the army which was recruiting for the Napoleonic Wars, and served in the Royal Artillery. Through a fellow soldier he came to faith in Christ. On returning to Shetland, probably in 1819, such was his evangelistic fervour and his concern for his native people that, in spite of failing health, he preached and held classes, planting Methodism in the hearts of the people. Nicholson appealed to the Conference to send preachers as the work grew apace and after a visit from one of the Edinburgh ministers who reported his findings to Conference two preachers were appointed. So John Raby and Samuel Dunn arrived in Shetland in 1822. They traversed the moors in the black night of winter when there were few made roads; the work continued to grow. By 1828 when John Nicholson died seven or eight chapels had been built and many other preaching places maintained. Six ministers were staffing four circuits and two or three thousand Methodists were meeting across Shetland. John Nicholson died at Gruting and a tombstone to his memory stands in the nearby cemetery. In 1922, the centenary of Shetland Methodism was celebrated by building a new manse at Gruting and naming it the Nicholson Memorial Manse. This was the manse to which Elizabeth came in 1967.

Eight

Shetland Isles

Shetland is about the size of the Isle of Man and the Isle of Wight put together. The mainland is long and narrow and at its southern tip lies Fair Isle from where many of the wonderful Shetland knitting patterns have come. This is twenty-three miles south of the mainland, midway between Orkney and Shetland. It now belongs to the National Trust for Scotland and accommodation is available in the bird observatory for visitors, whether bird-watchers or not. A beautiful island with a sheltered harbour, I visited it once with the ladies' knitting guild from Gruting. Being a poor traveller and flying in a small inter-island plane, I took a couple of travel sickness tablets, not realising how short the journey would be. As we had our meal in the bird observatory I found myself falling asleep so sent my friends on ahead to explore the island whilst I recovered. Hence I saw very little of this beautiful place.

Off the north-eastern tip of the mainland lie two more islands, Yell and Unst. Yell, the largest and next in size to the mainland is rather bleak and very peaty. Unst is quite an attractive island and just beyond it lie the jagged rocks of Muckle Flugga with its lighthouse to mark the most northerly tip of the British Isles. To the east of the mainland lie the inhabited islands of Fetlar, Whalsay, Out Skerries and Bressay. There are, in fact, over a dozen inhabited islands. When we were there the total population of Shetland was around seventeen thousand but with the discovery of oil more people came to work there and the population rose to about twenty-six thousand. Some of them have stayed, preferring a more peaceful way of life. I shall never forget a visit to Fetlar when we saw the snowy owl and her chicks. Sadly, I think there was a year soon after that when her mate failed to return so, possibly, there are no snowy owls to be seen on Fetlar now. The Out Skerries are two very small, inhabited islands joined by a bridge plus one other uninhabited island. These have a special place in our hearts as we have visited and stayed there several times. Our friend, Kate, had relatives there and so we were able to go and stay with them. On the first occasion the Church of Scotland missionary (a lay assistant) was away and we were asked to conduct Sunday worship. On our next visit, as we walked around the island the people were asking, “Will you be taking the services?” We couldn’t as we were not staying over the weekend, but on our third visit we discovered that the missionary had been told that he wouldn’t be needed and so we gladly officiated again!

To the west of the mainland lie the inhabited islands of Papa Stour, Vaila, near Walls, and Muckle Roe which now has a bridge across to the mainland. By far the most remote of all Shetland’s inhabited islands is Foula, lying way out west and often visible on the horizon. Though not as far from the mainland as Fair Isle it is often less accessible due to the weather. We did visit the island, but until the day of the proposed visit dawns one can never be sure of the trip; the mist has a habit of descending on Foula quite quickly. Since the evacuation of St. Kilda this is now the most remote inhabited island in Britain.

One of our island visits was to the lovely Papa Stour. Walking around the cliffs and across the island we managed to collect enough mushrooms to meet our needs for weeks afterwards. But here an unexpected wonder awaited us. Suddenly we saw an eider-duck, evidently disturbed by our approach, moving in a direction in which she obviously wanted to lead us. We made our way to the spot she had left and caught our breath at the most wonderful sight of her nest. It was all of pure down plucked from her breast. About ten to twelve inches in diameter, its walls were about two inches thick, and it contained a clutch of light green eggs. We took our photographs as quickly as we could so that we could move away and allow the eider duck to return.

Two uninhabited islands to the east of the mainland are rather special and a must for visitors. One is Noss, just off Bressay, now a nature reserve. It is reached by taking a ferry to Bressay, walking two and a half miles to Noss Sound, unless you are able to hire a car, and whistling or calling to the shepherd who lives there during the Summer months; he will then row across in his boat and take you to the island. From the shepherd's cottage near a sandy beach the isle slopes upward to the Noup of Noss where a sheer cliff plunges six hundred feet to the sea. In the breeding season every ledge and cranny is occupied by fulmars, kittiwakes, puffins, razorbills, guillemots and gannets. The lower slopes are the breeding grounds of great and arctic skuas which dive to attack you if you venture too near. It is advisable to carry and hold aloft a strong stick to protect yourself. If a visit to Noss is not possible a launch can be hired from Lerwick to take you round the island and take you close enough to the cliffs to get some spectacular camera shots. To see the gannets take off, fold back their wings and dive, torpedo-like, into the sea is breath-taking.

The other island that must be visited is Mousa, again east of the mainland and not far south of Noss. Rising from the ground you will see a large circular stone tower with walls forty-three feet high and nearly twenty feet thick, a masterpiece of dry stone workmanship. The walls surround a courtyard twenty-two feet in diameter. “Whatever is it?” you may ask, “and why was it built?” These questions were asked for many years before study and excavation produced some answers. It is the best-preserved and most extensively-excavated pre-historic broch. Others are to be found in Shetland as well as in Orkney and the north of Scotland but some are reduced to heaps of rubble. Here, it seems, a whole community could live, sheltered from gales and safe from any invading force. Timber tenements lining the courtyard wall provided living accommodation and at ground level there was a central fireplace. We visited Mousa more than once and it was quite an experience to climb to the top of the broch and try to think back to the Iron Age.

Discovering Shetland would take a life-time and I had only six years there, but what a privilege those years were. My work as a deaconess was to be for one year but at the end of that year I had become immersed in Shetland life and grown to love it more. I did publish a few songs with guitar chords and I did enjoy my work in the schools and in circuit but felt there was much more to do there. So when the letter came toward the end of the year saying that a replacement minister had been found for the work in the Lerwick circuit I had very mixed feelings. Furthermore, it seemed that there was still no evangelistic appointment for me. I must say that the Warden did his utmost to find such an appointment and there was a very protracted correspondence between us. However, when I was asked to have charge of twelve churches on the Welsh border I knew that I could not agree to go. I also knew that if I could not accept the discipline of the Order the only thing to do was to resign. I hadn't envisaged this and neither had the Warden, but this is, in fact, what I did. The President of Conference who visited Shetland that year expressed his view very strongly that I should not have had to resign but that I should have continued as a deaconess in sector ministry. Quite a number of ministers in secular jobs were then doing this kind of work. However, my appointment in Scalloway had come to an end and the manse had to be vacated so I moved across to Gruting and shared the manse with Elizabeth. Though there was a good deal of heart-searching this was to prove a very happy and fruitful time.

Nine

Shetland Life

Travelling to schools from Gruting and returning there in the afternoon was simpler than working from both Scalloway and Gruting. The manse was little more than a crofter's house but we made it cosy and welcoming. Sitting by a peat fire, especially on those wild, stormy nights was a real delight. We also kept in a good supply of peat for the Rayburn in the kitchen.

Cutting and curing peat took up a good deal of time throughout the year. Willie from the hamlet of Culswick, a crofter and a member of the little chapel there, became a very good friend to us. He gave us the use of one of his peat banks and also organised a team of men to cast (cut) the peats each year. In preparation for this work, usually in March, the banks were flayed, which means that the turf was sliced from the surface of the bank with a large spade. A line was first cut through the surface of the turf, parallel with the face of the bank and about twelve inches in, with a ripper. This was a blade about eight inches long set at the bottom of a long wooden shaft and at right angles to it. The sharp edge was on the outside so that it could be pushed through the turf.

The casting day was in May and Elizabeth made sure that the men came on the first Saturday each year and that there was plenty of food to keep them going. We took their elevenses to the hill and they came to the manse for lunch. Although it was a very substantial one they went back to the hill afterwards to cast more peat and then returned to the manse for more refreshment. The tool they used for casting, the tushkar, had a long wooden shaft as did the ripper but the blade was a specially designed L-shaped blade which, when pushed down into the peat, would cut a block the size of a brick. This was carefully lifted and placed on the bank. Each of the five men would cast several thousand peats so you can imagine the sight as they were carefully stacked to allow the air to circulate and begin the drying process.

About three weeks later they were dry enough to be handled so then came the raising of the peats when they were put into small pyramids, leaving gaps to enable further drying. After another three weeks came the turning of the peats when they were put into larger pyramids. All this work of raising and turning was done by the women, so we had our share in it too, though friends and neighbours often helped each other. Elizabeth would be up and on the hill at six o'clock in the morning so that she could start her day's work by nine o'clock. Who said anything about Shetland life slowing her down? I did when she first told me of her appointment. But, of course, I was wrong.

Raising and turning peats was good, healthy work and all the more enjoyable when the sun was shining and the skylark singing. Though the peats would come to no harm standing on the hill, most people would want to get them home and build a stack to have them more accessible through the winter. Some weeks after the turning of the peats we were loading up Willie's tractor. There were a few occasions when it got bogged down on the hill, but eventually the peats were off-loaded outside the manse. We usually had visitors through the summer and they were delighted to lend a hand in building the stack. This was a job of some skill. The broken pieces and blue clods, which were the harder and longer lasting pieces, were put into the middle of the stack. The pieces from nearer the surface of the hill were kept for the final layers to give some protection. All was built in such a way that the rain would easily run down the outside of the stack and so the rest of the peats would be kept dry. We usually had so much peat that we were able to store some in part of the garage and still leave room for Elizabeth's car.

Though I gave a hand in curing the peat my main outdoor work was the garden and looking after the hens. Those days in the garden were so enjoyable and it was a time of new discoveries. What would grow well in a peaty soil? How did the climate affect the growing season? These and other issues were resolved largely through trial and error. The soil was good and there was no shortage of manure with the sheep and hens around. I was introduced to the Shetland black potato that grew well there, and I was able to grow enough vegetables for our needs throughout the year. As I mentioned earlier, the high winds prevented the growing of tall crops such as runner beans, but we had plenty of root vegetables. The two cold frames that I had made from old windows served very well to bring on crops that bit earlier than would have been possible otherwise.

The hens were a joy to have around, adding their clucking sounds to the bleating of the sheep and the calls of the birds. I had made it possible for them to go through the closed gate at the bottom of the garden and enjoy the freedom of the hill, so we also had the taste of free-range eggs. I loved to go and collect the eggs from the nesting boxes and sometimes they were still warm. Any eggs that we didn't want to use immediately were preserved by Elizabeth in isinglass. We learned more in Shetland than anywhere else about being thrifty and self-sufficient. And why not multiply our stock? After all, we had a cockerel so could use our own fertilised eggs. The trouble was that we never seemed to have a hen go broody. But the problem was not insurmountable; we could borrow a broody hen from a neighbour, and we did. But where was the maternity unit to be? Lily, a friend from Skeld and a steward of the chapel there was a very practical person who had her own fishing boat, though she was getting on in years, and it was she who came up with a solution. She offered us the use of a very large barrel and this was placed on its side in the garage. Through the specially made opening we placed the eggs on a bed of straw and soon the broody hen was sitting comfortably. So far, all had worked a treat. It was a very exciting few weeks as we waited for the eggs to hatch. During this period we had a friend staying with us, Eileen, with whom we had shared some caravan mission days in Yorkshire. One evening, as she and Elizabeth sat talking late into the night, she suddenly noticed my absence and asked where I was. “Oh I expect she’s on midwife duty,” replied Elizabeth, and so they both came into the garage to find me patiently sitting by the barrel. Our patience was finally rewarded and we found ourselves proud owners of a dozen beautiful, fluffy chicks, that is, after they had grown a few feathers. Mother hen was very proud, too.

Our next visitors were my mum, dad and gran who had all come up to Shetland by plane. I think for all of them it was their first trip by air. We enjoyed taking them out and showing them some of the wonderful places in Shetland But the work went on: my main task was making a run for the chickens and it was gran, practical as ever, who was keen to lend a hand. She was a great help, especially in measuring and cutting the lengths of wood. Soon we had the chicken wire stretched across the top and the chicks installed.

There were various breeds of hens in Shetland but the one that had taken my eye was the tappet (or topped) hen, so called because of its top-knot, a small, white bird and very attractive. One crofter who had some promised he would bring a few over for me and, sure enough, not many days later, he arrived at the manse. On this occasion Elizabeth’s parents were staying with us. Elizabeth was baking and we were generally engaged in household tasks. Before we could give our attention to the new arrivals their owner had tipped them out of the sack in which he had carried them and scattered them amongst our Rhode Islands. Furthermore, one of the new arrivals was a cock, which didn't seem a good idea when we already had a cock. What a furore there was! Some of our hens just ran and stuck their heads into the wire netting of the run, not realising that they were perfectly placed to give pleasure to the new cock. Others took off over the wall and ran up the hill and soon Elizabeth and I with our crofter friend were in hot pursuit. Elizabeth's mother then emerged from the house to tell her that the yeast was rising and she had better come. There was no way she was going to turn her attention from hens to yeast. Nor did she until we had caught the last escaping bird and all were safely back on home ground. Having settled our own stock first we were then able to introduce the newcomers gradually. Well, it was a new experience and part of the rich tapestry of Shetland life.

Elizabeth had settled into Shetland life from the time of her arrival there. She had wondered what the reaction of the men would be when she took her first funeral, but there was total acceptance. In those days women didn't attend funerals but waited at the house whilst the men went to the service and committal. Elizabeth's pastoral care was very much appreciated by all the people in the area; she visited not only those of her flock but those of other persuasions and those of none. Soon she didn't need to knock on any door for she was expected just to walk in and the people were glad to see her. People were very caring, keeping an eye on the manse to make sure the lum was reeking, especially when she had the enteritis.

Most crofters had their own fishing boat and often came along with haddock or mackerel or other delicacies. Joe from Skeld was one of these and offered to take Elizabeth out in his boat to catch a few fish. It was a bail as you go job as his boat was rather leaky, but she enjoyed it. When I joined her at Gruting I was also invited to go with them. When we reached the herring grounds we each had our reels at the ready and let out a few yards to tempt the herring. As soon as we felt the tugs we hauled them in and took the fish off the hooks. At least, Joe and I took the fish off the hooks as that was the only part Elizabeth couldn't do. I was really impressed at the tremendous catch we had, so much so that it had a mention, as follows, in one of my little ditties.

Out at the flays with Joe one night
In Summer-time,
Thirty-one haddock took a bite,
Hooked on my line.

We sang this at one of our local concerts to the tune of "Li'l Liza Jane".

Of course, the fish had to be cleaned and gutted before they were put into the freezer and this could be a very time-consuming job. Prior to my arrival in Shetland two couples, Ann and Alan and Jean and George who were friends of ours, had a holiday with Elizabeth and they, too, went out fishing. They hauled in a tremendous catch of mackerel and were gutting fish well into the night. Well before the end was in sight Alan was heard to say, in sheer desperation, "Could we not resuscitate these?" But they saw the task through and thoroughly enjoyed the fish meals that followed.

In the Gruting manse there was a harmonium so it had a good airing when I joined Elizabeth. The Superintendent minister lived in the Walls manse, about four miles away, and when John Hirst was appointed we soon became friends with him and his wife, Agnes. Each Sunday evening, after the day's services Agnes and John would come over for supper. Agnes was a contralto and enjoyed singing so we would spend some time around the harmonium. Then John had a brainwave. Organists were in short supply in some areas and others were not eager to attempt certain tunes. "How about making recordings to be used in services?" he asked. Soon the venture was underway. John had chosen sets of hymns for particular services and these we recorded as the four of us sang to the harmonium. I believe they were used for some years after we had left Shetland.

Our foursome led on to others joining us and soon we had a singing group. We decided we had better have a name and after some deliberation reached the decision that "The Accidentals" would aptly describe those who could come rather than those who could sing!

It was on one of the evenings when Agnes and John were with us that we had a phone call from another crofter to say he had something for us which he would leave on his way home from fishing. Soon we had a box of squirming crabs in the kitchen. "Can you deal with these?" I asked Elizabeth. "What do you do with them?" she enquired. "Boil them alive", I replied. "Oh no", she said, "could you?" "No," I said. So we asked a favour of Agnes and John who passed near the sea on their way home. “Would you be able to take these crabs and put them back in the sea?” They kindly agreed and so that was the last we saw of the crabs.

Not only did we do well for fish in Shetland, but we also enjoyed heather-fed lamb with its own distinctive taste. Tom, who was one of our preachers and a crofter, said he would bring us a couple of lambs and show us how to butcher them. He was as good as his word and arrived one day with the lambs already skinned and ready to be prepared for the freezer. One lamb was left in the bath while the other was placed on the kitchen table. With hatchet and sharp knives at the ready Tom prepared to show us the art of butchering. In fact he carved up the first lamb for us and left us to do the other one. But what a state the kitchen was in with splinters of bone and pieces of lamb all over the place. So our first job was to tidy up the place before we began to practise our newly-learned skills! I think we could say we did a successful job on the second lamb and perhaps had less mess to clear up than after Tom’s efforts. But we were grateful for his help and how we enjoyed the taste of Shetland lamb. No other ever tasted so good.

Marjorie was another soothmoother. She had taught in Germany for many years but was now looking after her father in a cottage by the sea. I think she rather envied the Shetlanders their simple faith but couldn’t take it on board. She attended some services at the chapel and when I preached there on ‘assurance’ had quite a few questions and comments. How I would have loved to see her take a step of simple faith but this intellectual had many doubts and queries. I think in some ways she tried to emulate the Shetlanders. Was this why she came to have a rowing boat? She did so want to take us out in this boat and promised to stay well in towards the shore. After months of asking we finally agreed. It was a good day and as we set off, Marjorie had the appearance of an expert oarswoman. She was certainly enjoying herself and so were we. After some time I posed the question, "Marjorie, could I row for a while?" Well, it wasn't the easiest manoeuvre to change over mid-stream, as it were, but she agreed. The slight rocking of the boat was nothing compared to what followed. Suddenly we slipped an oar. Over the side it went and, though fully clothed, Marjorie dived in after it. To avert further disaster she refused to try getting back into the boat but passed us the rescued oar. So with Marjorie hanging on at the stern we rowed back towards home. On arrival the first thing was to get Marjorie into the house to wash and change and warm up. Her appearance was that of a drowned rat, but amazingly she suffered no ill-effects of the experience. I don't think we did either but it was our first and last trip in Marjorie's boat!

12. Replica of a Viking ship in Lerwick

13. Foula, looking from west side of Shetland

14. Elizabeth on Mousa, near well-preserved broch

15. Janet with friends on the Skerries, showing the bridge joining the two islands together

Ten

Clouds across the sky

We still look back to Shetland and feel that it was one of the happiest times of our lives, but, of course, a few dark clouds will sometimes drift across the brightest sky.

One evening the phone rang. It was my brother-in- law, Gray. "I'm afraid I have some bad news for you, Janet," he said. My brother, Graham, had suffered a massive heart attack and died. Well, it was a huge shock. Graham left a wife and five young children. It was at times like this that one was aware of being so far away from family. I knew they all would be walking through a dark valley, but I felt so deeply for mum. Graham was her blue-eyed boy and she had always doted on him.

I sat down and, of course, committed everything and everyone to the Lord. Elizabeth was a tower of strength and I was so grateful for her presence and support. At two o'clock in the morning we still had no thoughts of bed, but I began to write down the words I felt God was giving me and I include them here:

Deliver Us Lord!

Deliver us, Lord! Such is the cry
From hearts that are overborne
With sorrow and care and the things of this life
Which crush us and make us forlorn.
Deliver us, Lord! We often ask
To be free from the burden and strife,
To be those whose path is as smooth as silk
As they walk through a carefree life –
Perhaps not in so many words – but still
We would wish for our sea to be calm
With friends who are sharing the voyage with us
Kept safe and free from all harm.

Perhaps for some this is how things are
With so little of personal grief,
But if this is so then they hardly can know
Of the blessings of peace and relief
From the God of all grace Who is one with us,
Who in Jesus shared all that we share,
Who wept at the grave of Lazarus
And whose heart on the cross was laid bare.

What right have we then to ask to be free
From life's trouble and turmoil and test
If we're following the man of Calvary -
He knows what will bring out the best,
What will purge and refine and keep us near
To His heart which was pierced for the world,
What will make us more ready to share with all men
His comfort and peace which enfold
The needy, the empty, the trusting souls
The ones who will take from His hand

The cup, be it filled with sorrow or joy
And believe that their pathway is planned.
So it's all in His hands and we've nothing to fear.
Deliver us Lord? No! instead
Let us ask Him to keep us in all that we face,
Let us ask by His love to be led

Do you know what a privilege Jesus has laid
On the souls who pass oft through the fire?
What a trust he has placed in His children who lose
As it were, their heart's deepest desire?
Think of Job and those like him who in trial and flood
Believed in the goodness of God.
"Though He slay me I'll trust Him' – such courage and hope
When they felt they were under the rod.
But we know the God who in Jesus has loved
With a suffering, self-giving love,
So we'll trust in that love, though perplexed we may be
For He'll bring us to heaven above.

Janet I Edwards

The next day I made preparations to go down to the family and was able to spend some considerable time with them before returning to Shetland. The Education Authority there were so very understanding and helpful. It was hard to leave mum; Graham's passing had struck her a powerful blow. When I arrived back in Shetland I found support and strength as I knew I would, but it was Elizabeth who carried me through those difficult days. When I couldn't sleep she recited poems, all known by heart, and Scripture verses that were so appropriate to my need. I think I learned a few of those poems, and ones like 'Silver' by Walter de la Mare and 'Nod, the Shepherd' still mean a lot to me.

There were, of course, silver linings as well as the clouds. My brass teaching in the Anderson High School meant that the town band was augmented, whilst running a few guitar classes meant extra links with some of the young people in the area. Each year there was a youth camp that catered for the young people across the Shetland circuits, and we became very involved in this. I well remember one of them that was at North Roe. The school-room floor was a bit hard for sleeping but I think I managed to secure a mattress from somewhere! Some brave souls camped out. We had a number of volunteers from the churches to help with catering and the general running of things. One or two also shared in leading prayers. Betty was a young woman from Lerwick who offered to come and help, just as long as we didn't expect her to lead prayers. I remember talking with Betty in her tent late into the night. She had possibly been searching for a personal faith but had never taken the step of commitment. That night she did and the change in her was soon very obvious. It has been a joy to count her among our personal friends. That youth camp was the beginning of a Christian journey for a number of young people.

As we travelled around Shetland we often saw sights that took our breath away. The wild life in particular was such as might never be encountered elsewhere. I was driving home one day when I noticed a flash of gold and a bird moving in the grass. I stopped the car and went back to see what it was. I had never seen one before but I knew it was a golden plover. She obviously had her nest there so I didn't stay too long. We walked over the hills with extreme caution in the Spring. So many tiny lapwing chicks would appear as if from nowhere and mother would not be far away. The oyster-catcher, too, had chicks across the moor, whilst on the sea-shore the arctic terns were raising their families. The wild-life was prolific and a trip around the coast would reveal hundreds of sea-birds on ledges of the rocks where families again were being nurtured. Yes, there were many silver linings but there were more clouds to come.

Mum never seemed to recover fully from Graham's death. She became poorly and was treated for some time for anaemia but on my visits home I could see her deteriorating. Eventually I was able to see the consultant and ask what the problem was. "Your mother has a disease from which she will not recover", he told me. "It could be weeks, months or a few years". The name he gave to it was lympho-sarcoma. He advised me to return to Shetland and try to live as normal a life as possible. He also said that I could telephone him whenever I wished. This was quite a blow but I knew I had to try and follow his advice. Of course, I telephoned regularly and he was so caring and helpful. Mum had regular visits to him and her need of blood transfusions became more frequent. Somehow I seemed to know when the time was right to go and look after her. However, on the day I was due to sail, taking my car down with me, there was a dockers' strike. This was rather unusual in Shetland and some of the office staff who knew my situation told me I needn't worry. They saw that the car was loaded on to the boat and I sailed south, again with the understanding and goodwill of the Education Authority.

At this stage mum needed looking after and I assured her that I would stay until she was well again. Over the next weeks she was to need nursing and loving care which I was privileged to give. It was hard for gran to see her own daughter slipping away. The knowledge that all was in God's loving hands was a source of strength but our hearts were aching. I remember driving behind the ambulance as she was taken to hospital for the last time and crying out to God, "Lord, if you are going to take her, please take her". That night He did.

Back in Shetland the pain lingered on and Elizabeth was again my tower of strength. The ache in the heart would grow less over the months but I felt there would always be one part of the jig-saw missing. Life in Shetland continued to be very fulfilling but we knew we couldn't stay there for ever. Eventually the time came when Elizabeth's work in Shetland was done and she received an invitation to visit the Tebay, Appleby and Kirkby Stephen circuit in Westmorland, soon to become Cumbria. There she would meet the circuit stewards and, if it seemed right, consider accepting their invitation to minister in the circuit. She had always felt called to the Methodist ministry but the way had not opened for women until 1973, so until then she had served as a Wesley deaconess. However, she was one of the first women to offer when the opportunity arose and was ordained as a Methodist minister in 1974. Her visit to Cumbria was fruitful and soon we were in the throes of packing. Having shared a home for four years we were obviously planning to move together. Not only did we have the usual goods and chattels but decided that we must take a few sacks of peat with us. We also had three cats. We had given away our hens and I knew I should miss them so much. Many farewells were said and all too soon we were boarding the boat for Aberdeen. The quay was lined with people from across the circuit and the boat seemed to take forever to turn ready for pulling away. We vowed that never again would we leave Shetland by boat.

Eleven

More a Continent than a Circuit

In September, 1975, we arrived in the Kirkby Stephen, Appleby and Tebay circuit, K.S.A.T. for short, where Elizabeth was to have oversight of the Tebay section. As we arrived at the Tebay manse I guess some people were filled with curiosity. Whatever could those thirty sacks contain? They had been off-loaded with a number of other things to await our attention. Perhaps they might guess when they saw and smelt the smoke of a peat fire. The manse was a terraced house that didn't conform to manse regulations, and the hope had been for some time to purchase one that did. However, we soon had a cosy home and to my delight there was even a small garden. We were there for a few years before another manse was bought. The Anglican vicarage was to be sold because of the joining of two parishes and the price seemed to fit the Methodist circuit budget, so the vicarage became a manse and our home for the rest of our time there. What a lovely house it was, a detached, Georgian style house with spacious rooms and a large kitchen with a Rayburn. We had plenty of room for meetings, committees, etc. But there was also a considerable amount of ground. It was a good job I was fond of gardening. Rose beds, borders, fruit bushes, large vegetable plots and undulating lawns filled a good many of my leisure hours. Those were the days when I had the energy as well as the enthusiasm. As we looked across the lovely Howgill fells we thanked the Lord for another place of beauty. Yes, of course we missed Shetland and we returned the following year for a holiday with our friends, Jean and George, but we felt we had come to the place of the Lord's appointing.

In one sense it was a strange move for me. After thirteen years in the deaconess order when I had been sent to my appointments here I was, not appointed or commissioned, but having to make my own decision about what I did next. The obvious thing, of course, was to look for a teaching post. A permanent post was not easy to come by but I did manage to get some supply teaching. The only savings scheme I had was a unit trust into which I had been putting twenty pounds each month, but I felt I should have to terminate this as I wasn't sure of what my income would be. Elizabeth was totally against this. "That is all you have towards retirement", she said. "You must keep it going and we'll manage somehow". Ministers' stipends were very low in those days and we had a large house to run, but we felt we must trust the Lord.

It was about two years later that I found myself at St. Andrews Boys' school in Penrith but after a year it was due to close and become part of a large new Junior school. The head of St. Andrews encouraged me to apply for a post in this new school where the head was looking for someone who would be able to teach music. So in 1979 I began teaching at Beaconside Junior School where I had responsibility for music. It was a large, open-plan school with over three hundred pupils on the roll and presented a new learning curve for most of us. I soon had two school choirs, one in the upper unit and one in the lower unit. The children really enjoyed singing and music making. Not only were they well used in school but also in the community.

But this was my day-job and my source of income. What about ministry? We were part of a very large, country circuit, then comprising over thirty chapels. I think it was an ex-President of Conference who had described it as more a continent than a circuit. The opportunities for preaching were many. In fact, I soon found I was out practically every Sunday as well as speaking at various fellowships through the week. In addition I was leading a youth fellowship and guiding two young preachers through their course of study. Music was also an important part of ministry and as I discovered a few promising voices in our local congregations we were soon singing together as a group. It was not long before we were being invited to conduct Chapel Anniversaries, Harvest evenings and other 'specials' in and beyond the circuit. Ten ladies comfortably filled two cars and into the boot we packed music cases, guitar, small keyboard and sometimes cornet. But what should we be called? We decided to call ourselves 'His Folk'. Our singing was usually in three parts and we practised each Wednesday evening at the manse. I had a bit of extra work to do in arranging the music and planning programmes, but we thoroughly enjoyed ourselves. This was part of our ministry and a blessing to many. In 1981 our first recording was made, entitled "Singing for Him" and later we did another, entitled "Songs for all Seasons". These, of course, were tape-recordings. They were well-received and quite a number were sold. The recordings were made by 'Reelife Recordings', Lancaster.

As well as music with 'His Folk' and music at school I also had a number of private piano pupils. Then I became involved with the Appleby Convention choir. This was a wonderful annual convention, very much on the lines of the Keswick convention and we had some excellent speakers, including some Keswick ones. The person in charge of the choir, however, wanted to hand over responsibility to someone else and the lot fell upon Jonah! So I became their conductor for a number of years.

Amongst all these commitments I found time to attend some advanced driving classes and in 1980 I passed my Advanced Driving test and have been a member of the Institute of Advanced Motorists ever since. I have always loved driving. I enjoyed driving the Renault 16 TS with its column gear change and then the Renault 16 TX but there came a time when it had to go. I remember I sold it privately for one thousand pounds. What next? I found myself outside Staveley Motors in Kendal looking at a second-hand Mercedes Benz 230 E. It was pouring with rain and I think the salesman really wanted to get home, but he took me out in it. As I drove back to the garage, Elizabeth said, "That's the car, isn't it?" I knew it was but had to talk business! I had no car, having sold it privately, so was hoping for an extra discount. The salesman was very obliging and I landed a good deal. What a wonderful car that was and excellent for transporting 'His Folk'. I should never have thought of looking at Mercedes Benz had not an evangelist who stayed with us driven off in one. I was quite surprised and asked him if it was not expensive to run. "No", he said, "it is the cheapest car I have ever run as it's not always in and out of the garage".

I think some people in the circuit raised their eyebrows. When I arrived at one of our country chapels to take the service I was met by Jeff, one of the farmers. "These teachers are doing alright", he said. "Ah, but Jeff, this is second hand; initially it belonged to a farmer", I replied. It did, a farmer from near Lancaster. I don't think I had any other comments from him. I kept that car for almost nineteen years and sold it privately, again for one thousand pounds. I shed a few tears as it was driven away.

We had in our area a Male Voice Choir and it was my privilege to be involved with them, sometimes chairing one of their meetings and sometimes writing songs for them. This was a choir that was part of the nationwide Male Voice Praise movement, so the programmes were always geared to the gospel. In fact, those wishing to join were told that there were just two requirements: the first of which was that they had a personal experience of Jesus Christ as Saviour, and the second was that they could sing! As I sat at the piano one day and a new tune was born for "My Jesus, I love Thee" I felt very strongly that it was for the Male Voice choir. This choir had strong links with the Glasgow Male

Voice choir, whose conductor, Bill Rodger, was the national secretary of the Male Voice Praise movement. He came to the Appleby convention one year when we were singing a song I had written especially for them, "Jesus, I owe it to Thee". "Janet", he said to me after the meeting, "I should love to have that song; could you put it into Male Voice setting?" Well, my songs had been written for soprano, alto, tenor and bass and I had never scored anything for male voice choir. So I asked him how I did it. "Oh", he said, "two tenor parts fairly close together and two bass parts fairly close together". So began my writing for male voice choirs. I think the first to go into their national song books was "My Jesus, I love Thee" and the second, "Jesus, I owe it to Thee". Normally I wrote both words and music and many others have followed, some of which have been sung by male voice choirs across Britain and Ireland. I have counted this a real privilege.

After nine years in Tebay, Elizabeth was contemplating a move but she was asked if she would consider staying on as Superintendent. This she did, which gave us another five years there. I was feeling that a change from Beaconside would be a good thing; the open-plan situation had never been my favourite thing. Sometimes it was like Paddington station with all the coming and going. We did, however, have a few uncrowded areas. There was an art bay, a language room in both upper and lower units and a music room. One day I was asked to take another class for R.E. whilst their teacher took my class to the baths. We looked at the story of Abraham, especially God's call to him. "How did he know God was speaking to him?" asked one child. We discussed this and I also said that I knew when God had spoken to me. The children wanted to know more about this but that wasn't the time or place to share my personal testimony, so I said that we could talk about it outside class time, possibly at lunchtime. The result was that we had another session later. This eventually led to quite a number of them wanting to begin the Christian life and there were some definite commitments that I knew had to be followed up. I talked to the head about this and he asked me what I would like to do. The result was that I began a lunch-time club for those who were interested and so "Friday Club" was born, which ran for some time. Often there was more questioning and discussion as well as time for singing and a brief prayer.

In 1986 I applied for a temporary headship of Warcop village school. It was for two terms and my job at Beaconside would still be there afterwards if I so desired. My application was successful and on 5th January 1987, I took up my new post. It was challenging but enjoyable. Quite a few cupboards needed sorting out, the P.E. store was a tip and a few discipline problems needed attention. At one parents' evening I was told by one lady, "Before you came I was thinking of removing my child from this school, but thankfully you have sorted out the bullying problems and things are much happier". I should have liked a longer spell there but I knew it was to be for just two terms. So, September 1987 saw me back at Beaconside, just in time to begin preparations with choir and musicians for

Christmas! It was that year that I spoke to William from Reelife Recordings about the possibility of doing a tape of the choir and in December 1987 he came and did the recording sessions in school. So our tape, "How far is it to Bethlehem?" was produced and quite a number were sold, especially to parents.

I was now thinking in terms of applying for further headships but I wanted to be sure of what God's will was. Computers were increasingly being used in schools and so one would have to be computer-literate, but the requirements for headships were changing in other ways; managerial skills were extremely important. Did I want to be a manager or a teacher? I think it was John Bird who was the speaker at our next Appleby convention and one thing he said was a clear word of God for me. His words were, and I think he was quoting from someone else, "If God has called you to be a preacher, never lower yourself to be a king". They translated for me into the following: "If God has called you to be an evangelist, never lower yourself to be a head-teacher". From then my thoughts were on giving myself even more to ministry.

So in 1988 I took early retirement. I knew income wouldn't meet outgoings but thought that I might be able to do the odd spell of supply teaching. I believed that, in any case, my needs would be met. For a number of years we had had a mortgage on a small, terraced house in Tebay. This had happened after some friends had bought a small house in Devon with the proceeds of a unit trust. We then wondered if my unit trust might be used in the same way. On discovering that it was worth four thousand pounds, which seemed a huge sum to us at the time and the like of which we had never possessed, our hopes were high. So we began to look around. But I wanted a very definite sign from God that we were to proceed. At this time, some friends from Yorkshire who often came up to stay in their static caravan and to preach in the circuit were paying another visit. We were rather taken by surprise when they asked us if they could make us a gift of the caravan as they were not going to be able to continue visiting the circuit for family reasons. They thought that perhaps we could use it for youth work or in some other way in our ministry. So the caravan became ours, and a local farmer agreed to move it and site it for us. Well, he did move it but before he was able to site and secure it properly a terrific storm smashed it to pieces. Nevertheless, we had seen this as a sign of God's provision and we took it as a sign to continue looking at properties. We looked in a number of villages before coming back to Tebay where there was a double-fronted terraced house for sale. From our chapel steward we learned that his grandfather had built this along with a few other properties, but this was for himself and the best materials went into it. We made enquiries, only to discover that there was already a proposed buyer, but that he was very slow in coming up with the deposit. We were due to go on holiday to Shetland and as we left I said to Elizabeth, "If it is right for us to proceed then the property will be there for us when we return from Shetland". Indeed, when we came home it was not long before the phone rang. It was the estate agent to tell us that the proposed buyer was still not forthcoming with a deposit and, if we liked, we could go ahead.

The next thing was to see if we were candidates for a mortgage. The Bradford and Bingley building society agreed to give us a mortgage but on both salaries, not on one; my income at that time was still a little erratic. We were delighted, though there were many occasions when we wished we hadn't a mortgage. Some years our holidays were either staying with friends or borrowing a friend's caravan. But we were to see, much later, how right it was for us to buy the property in Tebay.

1989 was moving year and Elizabeth's next appointment was to be in Devon. She was invited to become Superintendent minister of the West Devon circuit and the manse was a very nice bungalow in Okehampton. Again, this was a wide, country circuit as three circuits had united to become one. And again, we were moving to a very beautiful area.

1989 was also the year when the Methodist Conference was to meet in Leicester and Elizabeth was a representative. She was expecting that I would travel down with her, not to attend Conference, but because we should be staying with Jessie, a very dear friend. At first I said "No" because there was plenty to do, especially in the garden, so that all could be ship-shape for the arrival of the incoming minister. However, in the end I gave in. So while Elizabeth was in Conference, Jessie and I enjoyed each other's company. One of the first things we did was to go out for a celebratory meal.

When I awoke in the middle of the night I had severe chest pains and began to wonder if I had eaten too much. I reached for my bottle of Maalox which was usually nearby but there was no relief there. Soon Elizabeth and Jessie were at my bedside and Jessie promptly sent for the doctor. His diagnosis was heart attack and in no time at all I was in the George Elliot hospital in Nuneaton. The prognosis was not good. Apparently Jessie was told, "We have all the right technology but we don't think we can save her". Jessie is a very practical person who thinks and plans well ahead so, in passing on the news to Elizabeth she asked, "What will you do Elizabeth? Will you take Janet back to Cumbria or will you have the funeral here?" I learned this later, of course. The next day I became aware of what was going on around me. I reached for my Bible and it fell open at the Psalms. I began to read Psalm 118. Verse 17 seemed to stand out from the rest as being just for me: "I shall not die, but I shall live, and recount the deeds of the Lord". What wonderful words. I have them underlined in my Bible. From then it was a steady recovery. We had travelled down in my car, the Mercedes, and the plan had been for Elizabeth to get a lift into Conference each day. But in the circumstances she had to drive the car into Leicester. When she came into hospital and told me of her exploits I replied, "That's enough to give me a heart attack!" From hospital it was back to Jessie's, so Elizabeth had to drive the car home until I was well enough to travel and then come down again for me. Then of course she had to cope with all the preparations and packing for removal as well as looking after me. But with help from friends all the necessary things were done. We are just twenty years on from that time and many more miracles have happened.

Perhaps one of the things that made leaving Tebay a little easier was that we already had friends down in Devon. But pulling up one's roots is never easy. I knew I should miss 'His Folk' and there were people I should miss too, but we should doubtless be back.

Twelve

The West Devon Circuit

Lois was the circuit steward in Okehampton with whom Elizabeth had already been in touch during negotiations about the appointment. She was a widow, occupying a bungalow overlooking the town centre, always busy and always looking for ways to help other people. She was already looking after the out-going minister's wife who was recovering from eye surgery but she was happy to accommodate me for some days while Elizabeth organised the move. So Elizabeth drove me down in my car, returned to Tebay by train and, having organised the furniture van, drove down to Okehampton in her own car.

My hopes of doing some supply teaching were now rather fragile, though, as the weeks went by I seemed to be making a fair recovery. I was able, again, to take a number of piano pupils which I enjoyed. I was also assessed to see if I qualified for any financial assistance and the outcome was that I began to receive invalidity benefit, so, again, my needs were met.

We were given a list of doctors at the local surgery so that we could make our choice. This we did and I soon learned that the one I had chosen had a special interest in cardiac related matters and visited Exeter hospital each week to be involved in this area. So that gave me extra confidence. The medical care was excellent but on 18th February, 1990, I found myself being rushed into hospital as a result of another heart attack. As I lay in the ambulance I looked up to the window above me. The lower half was opaque, green in colour, so that nothing could be seen through it, but the upper half was clear and through it I saw a beautiful sunlit sky. The words of the apostle, Paul, in 1 Corinthians, chapter thirteen, came to me: "Now we see through a glass, darkly, but then, face to face." It was wonderful to know that whether I came back to Okehampton or was taken to heaven I was held in God's loving hands. I thank Him for those who encouraged me to read my Bible daily. So much of it becomes part of us and God is able to remind us of those words that are appropriate to our needs. So I was able to relax and, again, I made a steady recovery.

When I returned home it was another new learning curve on how to pace myself. I wanted to be active and I wanted to be involved in ministry. One thing that I found relaxing and enjoyable was flower-arranging. I attended classes for this and learned a lot which I have found useful over ensuing years. In my enthusiasm I did a number of arrangements at home but, in giving them their daily spray, I nearly ruined Elizabeth's antique games table. The next classes I attended were furniture restoring classes and I took the games table to the class! I was horrified when I was told to apply Nitromors varnish remover, thinking it would destroy the lovely chessboard markings. But, of course, all it did was to remove the old polish and dirt. Then came another stiff challenge, the art of French polishing. There were three more classes before we were due to visit Tebay. Was it possible to complete the task? I must say that I was absolutely amazed when my efforts produced such a wonderful result. The table looked as good as new, better, if anything, than before. I was really proud to take it home and present it to Elizabeth.

As I became stronger I was eager to do a little more in the garden. We had a good vegetable plot at the back of the house and around the front a lawn and borders of shrubs. This had been laid out by a professional gardener, and there were some lovely shrubs. So I learned much about the care and pruning of shrubs. Ralph was one of our elderly preachers who was also quite a keen gardener and we were so grateful for all the help he gave us in the garden during our time in Okehampton.

But what of ministry? Another wide, country circuit with only three ministers meant that local preachers, too, were used to the full. I was soon preaching fairly often. In the circuit meeting concern was expressed that churches were not having communion services as often as they should or would like to have. There was need for someone to be given a dispensation from Conference to administer communion in addition to the ministers. My name was suggested by one of the preachers and the meeting agreed. So I was given a dispensation as I had often had before and I was happy to do this. Later, I had the privilege of helping younger preachers and met regularly with one preacher in training whose supervisor I became. I think we both enjoyed our time together as we talked about sermon construction and preparation of services and leading worship.

It was Alan Kinsey, one of the circuit ministers, who said to me one day, “Janet, you are a deaconess: you should be in the Order.” I had already been in touch with headquarters about receiving the prayer bulletin. At this time a number of deaconesses were being reinstated in the Order, for example, those who had married or gone into other work. It was suggested by the Warden that I might do the same and so I found myself in Birmingham for an interview. I agreed to be reinstated if I could be used, even if that meant being appointed elsewhere than Devon. The Order agreed to my reinstatement but it was felt that, because of my health record, I should not be sent into an appointment. So I became, again, a full member of the Order and able to share in its life more fully. It was good to be able to attend Convocation again and meet up with others I had known as well as taking a more active part in the life of the Order.

I thought heart attacks were behind me but on 1st October, 1992, whilst shopping in Newton Abbot I began to feel ill. I didn’t think it was a heart attack as it was quite unlike the others but my condition worsened and again I found myself in hospital. When eventually the consultant saw me he made it quite clear that the next step was bypass surgery and said it should have been done before. So I waited for a bed in either London or

Oxford. These times in hospital were not times of stress or anxiety but rather of rest and relaxation as I knew myself to be held in God's loving care. Earlier, a friend had lent me one of Marilyn Baker's tapes and I remember leaning back as if in the arms of God as she sang, "Rest in my love, relax in my care and know that my presence will always be there. You are my child and I care for you. There's nothing my love and my power cannot do". And also, there were many people praying for me, people in Cumbria, in Devon, in Shetland and in all the places where we had worked and ministered. That was such a blessing. Another great blessing was God's Word. My Bible was always beside my bed and one day I was reading from Paul's first letter to the Thessalonians, chapter 5. Verses 16 to 18 I found so stimulating and challenging: "Rejoice always, pray constantly, give thanks in all circumstances; for this is the will of God in Christ Jesus for you." I just had to put pen to paper and the following is what I wrote:

Meditation on 1 Thessalonians, Ch. 5, verses 16–18.

"Rejoice always, pray constantly, give thanks in all circumstances; for this is the will of God in Christ Jesus for you."

> Rejoice! Find joy and express it!
> In what? In my lot?
> In this world made beautiful and good
> But spoiled by man?
> Rejoice! This is the will of God –
> Find joy and express it!
> In what? In God, the faithful, mighty God

Who changes never – not even by a hair's breadth!
Who made you and loves you and will never let you go,
Who forgave you all that debt, the failure and the fickleness,
The resentment and the rebellion, the selfishness
And the sin against love.
Rejoice in Him!
Find joy and express it!
When? When I feel Him near?
When I see the clear tokens of His presence and provision?
On those occasions when I consciously bask in the warmth of His love?
Rejoice! Find joy and express it!
Not in the tokens of His presence but in Who He is!
Not in the blessings but in the Giver,
Not in the experience of Him but in Himself alone.
When? Not at times and seasons and festivals,
But always!
Rejoice always!
This is the will of God for you –
To find that joy and give it wings
In thoughts and words and prayers and praises,
In silent stillness, looking up to Him
Who is Himself your joy.
Always rejoice!

Pray! It is the invitation of love!
Pray! When should I pray?

Sometimes prayer is easy – at least words flow naturally,
But prayer is deeper than words;
It is a matter of the heart.
Sometimes no words are needed, so deep is the recollection of the presence of God.
Pray! Look to Him, listen to Him, rest in Him,
Walk in Him. Pray constantly!
Let it be your manner of life; it is so much more than an act or series of acts.
Pray! Live in it! Take deep, relaxing breaths of it,
Become intoxicated by it!
Swim in it; let it buoy you up and carry you along;
Dive deep into its glorious mysteries!
Pray, so that everything is a shared experience,
Yours and His.
Pray constantly!

Give thanks – it is to the Lord,
Who made you and loves you,
Who saves you and keeps you,
Who heals you and restores you,
Who deals with you gently, graciously,
And whose mercies are over all His works.
Give thanks – it is the only suitable response
For His great faithfulness and dependability.
Give thanks, not just when you feel like it,
But in all circumstances – and remember He is there.
Give thanks – for all the things that happen?
No, *in* all the things that happen.
The circumstances may not be the springboard of my praises

But they may be the field in which faith grows
As it is challenged and expanded.
We shall not be left to flounder in the maze of things,
We shall not be left to the mercy of storm and tempest,
For God is above circumstances,
So give thanks.
He is the Master-craftsman, the skilful weaver,
Whose design will be perfected.
He holds the world in the hollow of His hand.
Give thanks, not for the things that happen,
Nor yet in spite of them,
But let the overflowing praises of your lips and heart
Be the spontaneous result of seeing, beyond the circumstances,
The God of power and love.
In everything, give thanks!

Janet I. Edwards, October, 1992,
while awaiting heart by-pass surgery.

On 21st October, it was all systems go as two of us were transported to Oxford and were admitted to the John Radcliffe hospital. After examination it was decided to do my bypass at the earliest opportunity, which was the following morning. What a miracle, yes, another one. Five days later Elizabeth came to drive me back to Okehampton and to the District hospital where I was to be for almost a fortnight. That was a lovely, steady journey, and she had a tempting snack prepared for me. How wonderful it was to be going homewards again. I was not allowed too many visitors at first and I had to recoup my energies but I had excellent care in the hospital. Then, of course, it was home again and that was bliss. Apart from attempts to regulate my heart rhythm and a couple of cardioversions that weren't successful, I was back on the road to recovery.

In May, 1993, we had a lovely holiday in Jersey. Then in September we used Jean and George's house in Teignmouth while they were away. There was one night when sleep eluded me so I got up and went to George's keyboard. I found myself writing another hymn, "The Place of Peace", which eventually found its way into the Male Voice Praise collection. I feel that song-writing has been part of the ministry the Lord has given me. A book of carols has already been published. Perhaps there will be a book of hymns even though some have already been widely used by the Male Voice Praise movement. I think we used one or two in the circuit choir which I was able to form and conduct during our time in Okehampton.

Various classes were taking place at the college and when I learned that computing classes were at lunch time I suggested to Elizabeth that we might both take advantage of them. This we did and became fairly proficient at word processing, which has been a very useful skill.

Our five years in Okehampton passed quickly and 1994 saw us on our way to Lancashire where Elizabeth was to become Superintendent minister of the Great Harwood circuit.

16. "His Folk", our Tebay singing group

17. "His Folk" in action, Crossens chapel. Southport

18. Janet, on left, in her role as head teacher of Warcop Primary School

19. Janet practising for the All-Britain & Ireland Male Voice Praise festival – and her appreciative audience

20. Farewell to K.S.A.T. circuit

21. Okehampton manse. Janet building a retaining wall

Thirteen

Back to the North

Travel to Lancashire from Devon was vastly different from the days when Olive and I were on Caravan Mission work in Devon. Then we travelled up the old Fosse way and we should have been expecting nine to ten hours on the road. But the M5 and M6 had changed all that and the two hundred and seventy-five mile journey was accomplished in around four to five hours. So on 27th September, 1994, we arrived in Great Harwood, a small town which at one time had been in the very heart of the cotton mill industry and was known locally as 'Snuffy Arrod'. Those days were long gone and life was much quieter. The nearest sizeable town was Blackburn but Great Harwood itself was set among some attractive areas of countryside. There were two Methodist churches, two Anglican churches, one United Reformed church, two Roman Catholic churches and one Pentecostal. In the main street were quite a number of shops and so there was plenty of activity.

There were five churches in the Great Harwood circuit and Elizabeth had one other ministerial colleague. With a small band of local preachers all the Sunday services were usually catered for. I became part of the local preacher team but also found myself taking services in other independent churches, such as Congregational and Baptist. As Christmas approached there was talk of special events, Christmas concerts, etc., and again I found myself called upon to provide some music, so another circuit choir was born and I was able to use some of my own Christmas music.

One of the joys of returning north was the renewing of contacts made years before. My first deaconess appointment was Caravan mission work in Lancashire, beginning in the Clitheroe circuit. It was there that I had met Noreen and John who had become our friends. Noreen had made a commitment of her life to Christ in one of the meetings at Waddington so there was a special bond there. It is also a great joy to preach each quarter in that circuit.

One luxury I allow myself is a weekly visit to the hairdresser's, so one of my first tasks in Great Harwood was to find a hairdresser. This was before smoking was banned in public places and I knew that a number of people did smoke at the hairdresser's. Having been on a tablet for the heart, which made me rather chesty and had to be changed for another one, I knew I shouldn't cope very well if people around me were smoking, so I was looking for a hairdresser's where the problem could be addressed. I went into one salon to make some enquiries, and, of course, they wanted to know why I had the problem. What an opportunity! I told them about my health background, about the miracles, and soon a crowd of hairdressers were gathered around, eager to hear more. Again, God had given me an opportunity to witness to His love and power. I was assured that there would be no smoking when I went for my hairdo, so this became my hairdresser's.

There was a garden with the Great Harwood manse, not huge, but big enough for me to cope with. I thought, however, that perhaps I should have a more relaxing as well as enjoyable occupation, so I joined a local art class. It was a watercolour class, meeting weekly in Great Harwood. I had never tried my hand at watercolour but was eager to have a go. I found that I enjoyed it immensely and was eventually able to exhibit one of my paintings in a local exhibition. A couple of years later I became interested in calligraphy and began to attend classes. This, again, I found a fascinating craft and continued to enjoy it for some years.

In June, 1966, Lois from Okehampton came to stay. It was a busy time as we also had friends staying with us who were attending the Methodist Conference in Blackpool, as was Elizabeth. Lois and I were able to do our own thing. On 23rd June we went out together and on arriving home I had the most painful headache I had ever experienced. I jumped in the car and went down to the surgery. Later that evening the doctor was at the house and arranging for me to go into hospital. I think he knew it was a brain haemorrhage. Two days later I was transferred from Blackburn hospital to Preston where I underwent brain surgery. Then followed a period of complete rest as I was in a coma. Furthermore, my friends and relatives were told that I should not come out of it or, if I did, I could never be the same again. But our God is a God of miracles. Again, many people were praying for me. My nephew, Paul, came up from Derbyshire and offered what help he could to Elizabeth. I don't know how many plant pots he washed but he made himself busy and was a great help.

Elizabeth came to visit faithfully day after day. I had been telling her for some months that it was time she retired but it was the last thing she wanted to do. Now it looked as though she was going to have her hands pretty full with me if I ever came home again. One day as she sat by the bed she apparently said to me, "Janet, I will retire now." I have no recollection of this whatsoever as I was still in the coma, but she tells me that I immediately responded by raising my hand with a thumbs up sign! That, I think, is amazing and should make us careful of what we say to people who are very ill and apparently not responding to what is said to them. But what long days they must have seemed to Elizabeth. Almost a whole month passed, but then the miracle. I returned to consciousness and two days later the tracheotomy was removed: I was breathing for myself. As I heard the tea cups rattling on the tray which was being brought round the ward how I longed for a cup of tea, but that was not possible just then as I was still receiving food and medication intravenously. How long this continued would depend on whether my gag reflex began to work again. So when friends telephoned Elizabeth from Australia to ask what they were to pray for she said, "Pray that her gag reflex will work." Quite a lot of us had never even heard of a gag reflex before. Occasionally the doctor would test it, but it seemed to be a matter of 'wait and see.' One day Elizabeth came in, quite sure that it was back to normal, having received this assurance in her prayer time. She wasn't quite brave enough, however, to say so, but did ask if they would test it again. This they did and the miracle was confirmed.

Now followed a period of rehabilitation, learning to walk again and gaining confidence in performing tasks that to most adults are second nature. Each day that Elizabeth came in she would ask me to write something such as my name or a Scripture verse. At first it was so spidery it could hardly be read, but as day followed day I made progress and eventually what I wrote was legible. It was a long road back to normality. It was a wonderful day, though, when, on 23rd September I was discharged from hospital but the rehabilitation continued, due mainly to Elizabeth's loving ministrations. My doctor, a Muslim married to a Roman Catholic, said to me, "We have all been praying for you." And so, I was told, had the people in all the churches. We returned to the hospital soon afterwards to take in a box of biscuits for the staff of the ward where I had received such wonderful care. One of the nurses said to me, "I should like you to come with me and meet a group of patients who think they will never walk again." So we went to the rehabilitation ward. I was so pleased to be able to tell them of my wonderful recovery and to encourage them to be positive and hopeful.

The next year saw us holidaying in Devon again and in 1988 we visited Shetland. Elizabeth was as good as her word: she decided to retire in the year 2000 so we began to think about where we might live. She qualified for help from the Methodist Ministers' Housing Society but a certain percentage had to be found by us. So Helm house, our property in Tebay, went on the market. Prices had been spiralling downwards but even so, the house we had bought for nineteen thousand pounds sold for forty-nine thousand. We looked at properties in a number of areas but finally felt led to consider a small bungalow in Longridge. This was a very small town or, rather, overgrown village and, much as I wanted to be in the heart of the countryside, Elizabeth reminded me that we would need shops that were handy and we would eventually need public transport. Furthermore, Longridge was not too far away from the hospital in Preston and it had two good surgeries. But would our forty-nine thousand be enough for our input into the bungalow? Yes, it was – just. So, again, all was working out wonderfully.

Before our move from Great Harwood I had a request from Bill, the secretary of the Male Voice Praise movement: would I go and play the cornet, along with piano and keyboard, in the Male Voice Praise Festival being held in May, 2000, in Belfast, northern Ireland. Choirs would be there from all over Britain and Ireland. It was a festival held every five years. This time it was to be in the big, new Waterfront Hall in Belfast. Well, it was a privilege to be asked but I had to say, "Well, Bill, I haven't played much since the brain haemorrhage." His reply was, "We shall be singing two of your songs."

So I said I would consider it. When I received the programme from him it was a full programme for the Saturday evening plus a number of other items for Sunday morning services! One item, he indicated, would be introduced by a fanfare on the cornet. So I began my practice. I had never been to Ireland but had often thought I should like to go. We decided to make a holiday of it and went up a week before the festival began. The people in our churches in Great Harwood assured me of their prayers. "I should like you to pray for one thing in particular," I said to them; "speaking in public is no problem but when I play the cornet I can be a little nervous and that is not good for the breath control. Will you please pray that I don't get nervous?"

On arriving in Ireland I had to find somewhere to do my daily practice. On one occasion we stopped the car along a country lane and I got out and began to play. As I looked across the road I saw a herd of bullocks in a field. When they heard the sound of the cornet, they looked up and then moved forward as one for a few yards. This happened a number of times until they were at the gate. I said to Elizabeth, "That's the most appreciative audience I have ever had or am ever likely to have." The festival was a wonderful experience and a time of great blessing and exploring the Antrim coast was a great delight. We made a special trip to Dublin by train to see the Book of Kells in the Trinity College library. Soon after boarding the train I needed to make a phone call and as I used my mobile phone the gentleman sitting nearby must have heard my name. He came across to me. "Is it Janet Edwards who has been playing the cornet at the festival?" he asked. "Let me fetch my friend to meet you too." I felt like the queen! His friend was soon alongside him. "Have you any Irish money?" he asked. Well, no, we hadn't. Nor had we realised that we would need different currency from that used in northern Ireland. He was soon pouring coins into our lap and refused to take any money in return.

The holiday passed quickly and soon we were back in Great Harwood. I thanked the people for their prayers. "Your prayers were answered," I told them. "I'm not saying there were no blips but I didn't get nervous." Towards the end of May we were collecting the keys for our bungalow. Carpets had to be chosen and laid, shrubs had to be lifted and transported and, at the Housing Society's direction, some double glazing had to be done. My nephew, Paul, and his wife, Tammy, were insistent that they would do all the decorating and they did a wonderful job. So, August saw us moving into our own house, which we had never dreamed of owning, and a new superintendent minister came to Great Harwood, which was just half-an-hour's ride away from Longridge.

Fourteen

Life in the Ribble Valley

Longridge was a good choice. It had its own small supermarket and enough shops to meet most of our requirements. We soon linked up with the Methodist/United Reformed Church and were part of the Preston circuit. Preaching was again high on the agenda; in fact, I believe it to be my highest calling. Invitations came from independent churches and some preaching was undertaken in neighbouring circuits in addition to appointments on our own circuit-preaching plan. So life was again very busy, though I did try to exercise a modicum of caution as I was constantly advised to take things at a more gentle pace.

One of the first things, of course, was to visit the surgery and discover which doctor was to take me on. As I spoke with her she said she would like to do an E.C.G. When she had the result she came to me with a very worried expression on her face. "What's the problem?" I asked. "You can tell me; I've had lots of miracles." "Yes, I know," she replied. "It's heart block." "What does that mean?" I enquired. "It means your heart could stop beating at any moment," she answered. "So?" I ventured. "It means hospital," came her reply. "When?" I wanted to know. "Now," came her answer. So, again, I found myself in Preston hospital. It was a reasonably short stay but the outcome meant that I should probably have a pace-maker fitted fairly soon and this happened some time later. My initial reaction after the discovery of heart block was, "Well, Lord, all these miracles and now this blip." But, on reflection, I thought, "How wonderful; I didn't organise this but again the Lord had it all in hand."

We squeezed into our small bungalow but, having used one of the three small bedrooms as a study, there was little room for visitors, so this was rather disappointing. Another problem was that, having previously cut the library down by a third, getting rid of books which we had hoped to keep, we were going to have to prune again as we tried to find space in the new study for the rest. I can still see Elizabeth sitting in the study surrounded by boxes of books and looking more than a little downcast. In the end we had a further nine large cartons of books for which there was no space and these followed the others which had previously been sent to the Primitive Methodist Heritage Centre at Englesea Brook in Cheshire to boost their funds.

By the end of the year we were looking in estate agents' windows to see if there was anything with just a little more space. But being in a house that we owned jointly with the Methodist Ministers' Housing Society meant that there were certain restrictions. In fact, we discovered that the Housing Society was not prepared for us to move again under the same terms until ten years had elapsed! So, unless we could withdraw our share from the property and go it alone, the situation looked hopeless. But we made it a matter of prayer and trusted that God would guide us. Market prices rose and soon our house was worth much more than it had been when we moved in. But, of course, other houses were also costing more.

Quite out of the blue one day we had a telephone call from one of the local estate agents with whom we had talked and who knew our desire for a little more space. "I think we have the kind of property you are looking for," he said. "It is a three-bedroomed dormer bungalow. Are you interested?" Well, indeed we were and soon we were viewing the property in a lovely, quiet area, overlooking the town and some of the fells. The couple who lived there with two young children were all set to move further out into the country. We were very impressed with the house and the price seemed reasonable but when Elizabeth said to me, "Can we do it?" I had to say "No, we are about thirty thousand pounds short." A very dear friend who had also seen the house and thought it ideal said to us, "You will do it: you can have an interest free loan from me and pay it back as and when you are able." I said "Thank-you" and so we went ahead. The Housing Society put the bungalow on the market and were prepared to advance us seventy-five per cent of our share in the property but the other twenty-five per cent only after the bungalow had sold. We thought it would sell quickly but that was not to be.

But then another telephone call from the couple in the house we had agreed to buy. "This is Karl," said the voice. "I'm afraid we have pulled out of our contract on the house we were hoping to buy, for a number of reasons, and so we are not moving, though we are still actively looking and would still like you to buy our house." Well, that was a bit of a blow. Just when should we be able to buy their house? All seemed to be in the melting pot. But we had to remember that all was in God's hands. Karl was very apologetic but I told him that we should pray about it and leave it in God's hands as we did with everything. "Say one for us too," he replied. "Of course," I said, "we are all in this together." And so we waited and hoped and prayed and, of course, everything did work out. Having moved into Longridge in 2000 it was on 26th August, 2003, when we moved into our dormer bungalow.

A few days before, as we were working in the garden, a couple who lived nearby came to welcome us. "You move in on Tuesday, don't you?" they said. "Don't bother about lunch; we shall have it ready for you. Do you like salmon?" "Yes," we replied, and thanked them very much. On the day before the move we had planted shrubs in the front garden. When we arrived on the following day our neighbour appeared. "I have watered your shrubs," he said. "Thank-you," I replied, "that's great as I haven't yet got an outside tap." "Just use my hose," he replied, "whenever you want it." One of the great blessings of living here is the kindness of neighbours. So many had been so helpful to us that when Christmas came we held open house for them. The friend who had given us an interest-free loan was insistent that we first of all had double glazing done and only after that thought about paying our debts. We had quite a list of things that we wanted to do but it was going to have to be a gradual process. I had wanted a dish-washer but Elizabeth said that it was a good way down on the list of requirements and until we had paid our debts there was no way we could have one. The way things have worked out has been wonderful. Lots of jobs have been done and we are now clear of debt. We sometimes look around us and say, "How did this all happen?" We are so grateful to God who has loaded us with blessings and surprised us by His provision.

We are in the midst of some beautiful scenery; the countryside in the Ribble Valley is second to none. We have lived in some lovely places but we have never lived in an area with so many wonderful eating places where the food is so moderately priced. We enjoy classical concerts most weeks in a nearby village where the standard equals that found in any concert hall. The people are friendly and out-going. We believe we have been led to this time and place.

God still surprises me. Last year I put on weight but the problem was water retention. The doctor decided to send me for an echocardiogram and shortly afterwards I found myself at the heart failure clinic. I said to the specialist nurse in charge, "I don't know why I have come to see you." "Oh," he said, "as a result of your echocardiogram, which showed an enlarged heart, leaky valves and the left ventricle not performing as it should, but we are not going to let you go before your time." "You won't do that," I replied, "I've had too many miracles." "We want to avoid surgery if we can," he continued, "so we shall be increasing the strength of your medication." My energy levels have been very low and until recently I have felt no real improvement, but now I am feeling much better and it seems that the medication is working. A recent echocardiogram seems to confirm this. Had the doctor not decided to send me for that previous echocardiogram things might have been very different. But, again, I believe it has all been in God's plan.

As I look back over the past seventy-five years I am so thankful to those who in my early days focussed my attention on Jesus. I had Sunday School teachers whose lives gave evidence of His saving love and we had preachers in our chapel who made the gospel relevant. "So it isn't just since you were ill that you became a Christian?" asked one person recently. Indeed, no. I have been privileged to know God's presence from early days and though I have failed Him many times He has never failed me. The joy of serving Him and seeing others commit their lives to Him cannot be surpassed. Now I look forward to heaven, though, if God wills, once this book is published, there are a few projects yet in which I hope to glorify Him. After all, He is the God of miracles!